D0000886

Short & Sweet

Skits for Student Actors

55 sketches for teens

Maggie Scriven

MERIWETHER PUBLISHING LTD.
Colorado Springs, Colorado

Meriwether Publishing Ltd., Publisher
PO Box 7710
Colorado Springs, CO 80933-7710

www.meriwether.com

Editor: Arthur L. Zapel
Assistant editor: Amy Hammelev
Cover design: Jan Melvin

Library of Congress Cataloging-in-Publication Data

Scriven, Maggie.
    Short and sweet skits for student actors : 55 sketches for teens / by Maggie Scriven. -- 1st ed.
        p. cm.
    ISBN 978-1-56608-168-9
    1. Young adult drama, American. I. Title.
    PS3619.C7565S27 2010
    812'.54--dc22

                                                                2009051822

1   2   3   10   11   12

Dedication

This work is dedicated to the many people who have inspired
and encouraged me throughout the process:
My fabulous children Kendall, Carly, and BJ;
My friend Ryan, who was the inspiration for several skits;
My loving husband Chip.

Table of Contents

Preface:
The Play's the Thing

All Children Love to Perform

Throughout my years working with children both in dramatic productions and as a music and English teacher, I have found that most children love to perform. From the earliest ages, even the most shy children will join in with their friends in "putting on a play" for their friends or family and, with a little encouragement, they can overcome many personal obstacles through performance. This book is designed to help teachers, coaches, directors, youth leaders, or homeschool students approach drama in a simple, nonthreatening way with simple skits for young to middle school aged students.

Use Skits in the Classroom

The skits presented in this book were all written and used in a classroom setting. They require, for the most part, very little planning and, sometimes, very little memorization (readers theatre can also be plenty of fun). My experience has been that, through some of these simple skits, more than one reluctant student with shyness, disability, speech difficulties, or no previous experience whatsoever has become extremely excited about performing.

Let Your Students Direct!

I have specifically left the "direction" out of these skits, allowing the "director" (teacher or student) to interpret and arrange any emphasis, pauses, or characterizations. It can be incredibly rewarding to assign a more shy but responsible student to direct a skit. You will be surprised at the new level of comprehension he will gain of the art and the level of authority he will develop.

The Benefits of Classroom Drama

Although many schools are not fortunate enough to have comprehensive drama programs, I believe a simple addition of drama for a few minutes a week can effectively involve and address many needs for students. The benefits of drama for children are many, including building of self-esteem, public speaking, memorization, speech and elocution, and reading, along with discussion of moral issues addressed in several skits, including gossip, judgment based on appearance, and being the new kid. I used these skits to promote many different language arts and character elements and found that the students not only learned a tremendous deal and gained great respect for each other, they had a great deal of fun and looked forward to drama, almost without exception, as their favorite period of the week.

Use This Book As a Supplement

Although not meant to be used as a basis for a drama class, this book should serve as a terrific supplement to any adult who wishes to introduce drama to children in a fun and easy way without having to look through complicated and often inappropriate books of plays not written specifically for young actors. Each play in this book is totally G-rated and will be fun and easy for any group of students to perform and use for practice. Enjoy and break a leg!

Introduction

Casting a Skit

Many of these skits are not gender-specific. Although girls' or boys' names have been used, they do not specifically require a member of either sex, making this appropriate for single-sex and coeducational classes. In most cases, I did not elaborate on the personalities of the different characters. Although it may be easier to *typecast,* put the brainy student in the role of the brainy kid, this is also not necessary. Sometimes, playing against type is extremely enlightening to children.

I usually cast these plays by numbers. I would divide a class of sixteen students into four plays with four students. Randomly or by selection, the specific roles can be cast. If your students are responsible and work well together, you may allow them to select and/or cast a play themselves. This is easier to do in a smaller group. It is not unreasonable, however, to read through the skit and cast it with the students whom you see in the roles. Be careful about typecasting because it can be detrimental to a student's self-image. I did write these skits with, for the most part, specific students in mind. You may well find students who fit easily into these roles, but it is also a good idea to then recast the show, even with the same students in the opposite roles. This is especially fun in a two-person skit. Sometimes even the nicest kid enjoys playing the bad guy!

Staging a Skit

These skits were written to be read or performed during a short drama class. On occasion or for special occasions, the students were asked to memorize a skit and perform it for the student body or for parents. Be careful of expecting students to memorize, particularly if they are not good readers and/or good students. Although I absolutely do not think that drama should be allowed only as a reward for good students, you do not want to burden a struggling student with extra homework. It has often been my experience that students who do not enjoy or do well in school can excel in the performing arts. There is always a delicate balance between allowing them an excuse to miss homework in other subjects and requiring them to maintain a responsible level of achievement in their studies which should, of course, come first. This may be a discussion you will need to have with the students, your supervisor, or parents.

Most of these skits can be performed with the students holding the scripts and standing in front of the room and without any great movement. Memorization and *blocking,* the arranging of actors' movements around the stage, can come as the students become more familiar with a skit. Perhaps after many read-throughs of several skits, one or two are selected to be performed, and these can be blocked and memorized. Even for the most untrained and inexperienced actor there are a few basic blocking rules:

- Only cross in front of another actor when that actor is not speaking.

- Always keep your head out to the audience when speaking. Never turn backwards or completely sideways; this is called *cheating out.*

- All movement should look natural. Hand motions, etc., are at the actor's discretion and should never look like someone told him to raise his left hand on a certain line.

- Physical contact between actors — hand on shoulder, arm around friends, etc. — can be very effective in communicating feelings from the actors.

- I prefer to keep props to a minimum. In most cases, these will only cause a distraction and draw focus from the dialogue.

There are also a few basic rules about speaking on-stage:

- Speak *slower* and *louder* than normal. This is more of a challenge for some actors than others, but an invaluable lesson that can be used in many walks of life.

- Enunciate, enunciate! You may sound silly to yourself, but the guy in the back row of the theatre needs to hear every word. Don't throw away lines. Every line, particularly in a very short skit, is important to the plot and should be said to its advantage.

- Experiment on different ways to say the same line. Sometimes a simple emphasis on a different syllable can make a line sound much better, funnier, or more important. This is a good exercise to practice during class: Have the students stand in a circle and say the same line, one at a time, with different inflections in their voices and different emphases. A line to use might be, "What are you doing here?" For example, "*What* are you doing here?" "What are *you* doing here?" "What are you doing *here?*" Different emphasis can change the meaning.

Adapting These Skits for Elementary School or Special-Needs Students

Many of these skits deal with topics that can be enjoyed and appreciated by even younger students, although some of the vocabulary and cynical humor might be difficult for them to understand. It can be fairly simple to adapt some of these skits to be used for students as young as second or third grade, depending upon reading level, and may actually be an excellent tool as a reading exercise in class.

Almost all of the skits may be adapted, names changed, genders adjusted, and language simplified in order to be more accessible to elementary school students as well as older special-needs students. These may also provide an excellent editing and writing exercise for middle school students.

Some Suggestions for Adapting Middle School Skits for Elementary Students

- *Shorten sentences* particularly if the skits are to be memorized and performed; one sentence is usually appropriate for students through elementary grades.

- *Change names* if younger students have trouble with the names. It is also fun to interchange the actors' or students' names with the names on the script. This personalizes the skit and helps the actors remember to whom they are speaking.

- *Change the humor.* Some of the skits include typical middle school sarcasm and humor, which younger students may not understand. Simplifying the language while maintaining the humor may prove a challenge, but younger students enjoy performing the skits even without all the subtleties of the advanced humor.

- I have included some *blocking* suggestions and line interpretations in many of these skits. These are for suggestion only and, in order to simplify these skits for younger students or special-needs students, the blocking may, for the most part, be completely eliminated. Students may stand in one place and read the scripts and still get the message across.

- Unless there are many cast members, the shorter the *length* of the skit, the better for the younger students. One to one-and-one-half pages is usually all that elementary school kids can handle to keep their attention and aid in comprehension.

• Against logic, younger students may often *memorize* better than they read. Working at home on memorization on their own or with their parents often affords a much more impacting skit. To aid in memorization, I recommend bringing a tape recorder to a rehearsal and have the students sit and read the script. Make copies for each cast member to take home. Remember listening to Barney songs one hundred times in one car trip? Mom will be very thankful that you have provided this entertainment for the car, and everyone in the family will be able to perform the entire skit for you!

• I strongly encourage *performing* these skits for parents or other classes, particularly for students who are not advanced readers. Good preparation and work done at home may allow them to perform well and help encourage reading and speaking in public. Rehearsing a script over and over reinforces reading skills and self-confidence. Often a poor reader may be an excellent actor and acting necessitates more reading!

• Often, middle school students who have worked on these skits make excellent *student directors* and crowd-controllers for younger students so that several rehearsals can take place simultaneously. This is a great opportunity for developing leadership and directing talents in the older students, and the younger students enjoy it as well.

Summing it Up

This should be fun! Although drama is, by no means, a simple process, it should also not be a grueling chore. Students have enough of that in the rest of their classes! Although discipline and control do tend to be difficult in drama class, the mere reward of performing should be enough of an incentive for most children. Threaten them with more math homework, and they should shape up quickly!

Break a leg!

1. New Kid

Topic: A friendly, kind girl tries to approach a new girl who is resistant, angry, and unfriendly.

Cast:

SUE: nice, pleasant, and friendly
LISA: hard-edged with a chip on her shoulder
MARIA
BONNIE
DALIA
BRAD
TODD
JULIE
BARBARA
WINNIE
DIXIE
MARTY
MIKE
DAISY
CORY
BITSY

1   (*LISA is sitting on a chair or at a desk Center, looking through*
2   *a school textbook. SUE enters from Stage Right and*
3   *approaches Lisa.*)
4   **SUE: Hi. Aren't you the new girl?**
5   **LISA: Who's askin'?**
6   **SUE: Oh, uh, my name is Sue.**
7   **LISA: Good for you.** (*Continues to flip through book rudely.*)
8   **SUE: You're Lisa, right?**
9   **LISA: You must be a genius.**
10 **SUE: No, um ... do you have Mr. Craven for math?**
11 **LISA: Yeah.**
12 **SUE: Well, just a word of warning: Don't walk into his room**
13   **late. He goes nuts when people walk in late.**
14 **LISA: Thanks for the heads-up.**

1 SUE: *(Becoming warm and friendly)* **And Mrs. Davey loves it**
2 **when you say, "Yes, ma'am." That will earn you a lot of**
3 **brownie points in chemistry.**
4 LISA: *(Pauses. Looks up accusingly.)* **What do you want?**
5 SUE: **Huh?**
6 LISA: **Why are you bein' nice to me?**
7 SUE: **What?**
8 LISA: *(Sarcastic)* *Huh? What?* **Don't you understand English?**
9 SUE: *(Unsure)* **Well, yeah, sure, but I don't know what you**
10 **mean.**
11 LISA: *(Closes book and gains an unfriendly demeanor.)* **Well**
12 **listen, girl, let me tell you how it is. I'm new. This is the**
13 **seventh school I've been to in five years. Every city is the**
14 **same and the kids are the same everywhere.**
15 SUE: **What do you mean?**
16 LISA: **I lived in Baldwin for about six months. The longest**
17 **six months of my life.** *(Action moves to a group of three girls*
18 *standing, giggling, and pointing.)*
19 MARIA: **And she calls soda** *Coke!*
20 BONNIE: **Her shoes look like something out of a department**
21 **store catalogue!**
22 DALIA: **I heard she had to repeat eighth grade because she**
23 **moves around so much. What a loser!** *(MARIA, BONNIE,*
24 *and DALIA exit.)*
25 SUE: **That's awful.**
26 LISA: **No big deal. And it's the same everywhere. People**
27 **don't want nothing to do with you unless you have**
28 **something they want. Like in Clawson.** *(Action moves to a*
29 *group of three students and LISA joins them.)*
30 BRAD: **C'mon, Lisa, you said your parents wouldn't be**
31 **home.**
32 LISA: **Yeah, but they'd freak out if I had kids drinking in the**
33 **house.**
34 TODD: **Who's gonna tell them?**
35 JULIE: **Don't be lame, Lisa. Gosh, I thought you'd want the**

1   chance to make a few friends.

2   LISA: I do, but —

3   TODD: But what? Your house is the only place we could use

4   this Friday. Let's do it. It will be fun.

5   LISA: I don't know.

6   BRAD: I told you guys she won't go for it.

7   TODD: Yeah, I must have been wrong. I thought you seemed

8   like a nice girl.

9   JULIE: Let's go, guys. I've got a new CD I want you to hear.

10   *(The three leave, LISA rejoins SUE.)*

11   LISA: They only want to be friends when they want

12   something from you.

13   SUE: *(Quietly, unsure)* I don't want anything.

14   LISA: Then why are you trying to be so buddy-buddy with

15   me?

16   SUE: Ummmm ... I don't know exactly.

17   LISA: Oh, you must be like the bunch from Davison High.

18   *(Action switches to a group of four students. LISA joins the*

19   *group.)*

20   BARBARA: You have to join our gang.

21   WINNIE: It's the best gang in the school.

22   DIXIE: Don't join the Clods. They're the worst.

23   MARTY: You'll be sorry if you join the Clods. You'll get in all

24   sorts of trouble.

25   LISA: I'm not sure I want to join a gang or anything.

26   DIXIE: Why not? You got something against gangs?

27   BARBARA: Yeah, you saying we ain't cool or something?

28   MARTY: You already talked to the Clods or something?

29   WINNIE: I'm telling you, Linda, you join those Clods and

30   you'll be sorry.

31   LISA: My name is Lisa, not Linda.

32   MARTY: Whatever. You joining us or not?

33   WINNIE: You got a car?

34   LISA: No.

35   BARBARA: Shoot, she ain't even got a car. What we doin'

1   wasting our time with her?
2 **DIXIE:** You're a loser, girl, you know that? *(LISA returns to*
3   *SUE and others leave.)*
4 **LISA:** I don't have any money or a car, so what do you want?
5 **SUE:** *(Hands up in self-defense mode)* **Honest, I don't want**
6   **anything. I was just trying to be friendly. I know what it's**
7   **like to be new and I thought maybe you could use a**
8   **friend.**
9 **LISA:** I don't have *friends.* I move around a lot and don't get
10   close to people. That's the way I like it.
11 **SUE:** *(Slightly sarcastic, but not unkind)* **Yeah, you seem like a**
12   **real chipper person.**
13 **LISA:** Hey, don't get too close and you can't get hurt. That's
14   my philosophy.
15 **SUE: How's that working out for you so far?** *(Long pause.*
16   *LISA looks away.)* **That's what I thought.** *(Sits next to or*
17   *across from LISA. Leans in.)* **Look, I don't want to get all**
18   **up in your business, but it doesn't hurt to have a couple**
19   **of friends, even if you're only around for a short time.**
20   **Everybody I meet adds something to my life, that's the**
21   **way I look at it. Avoiding people because you don't want**
22   **to get hurt doesn't sound like much fun to me.**
23 **LISA:** Yeah? What do you know about it?
24 **SUE: I just moved here last year from Minnesota. It was a**
25   **little hard making friends at first, but I'm glad I did.**
26   **Some of the kids here are pretty cool. And it's always**
27   **better than going it alone. We need friends to keep us**
28   **from going crazy.** *(Action switches to four students whom*
29   *SUE joins.)*
30 **MIKE: You new?**
31 **SUE: Yeah. Hi.**
32 **DAISY: Good to know you. I'm Daisy. This is Mike, Cory,**
33   **Bitsy. What kind of music you like?**
34 **SUE: All sorts. I love classic rock.**
35 **CORY: Dude. Classic rock is awesome.**

1   BITSY: There's a concert Friday at the Bonsai Club. You
2   wanna go?
3   SUE: I don't know. I'll have to ask my parents.
4   MIKE: No problem. Let us know and maybe we can meet for
5   a burger or something before. We all hang out at
6   Diamond's before the concert. It's kind of an every-
7   Friday thing. The parents don't seem to care too much.
8   Keeps us "off the streets," they say.
9   SUE: Sounds great. *(The four exit and action returns to LISA,*
10   *and SUE joins her.)*
11 LISA: Sounds like the kids here are pretty cool. Not so sure
12   they'll like me, though.
13 SUE: Sure they will. You just have to let people in.
14 LISA: Easier said than done.
15 SUE: Well, I can be your experiment. I'll even put up with
16   your rotten moods. Here's my most important piece of
17   advice: Avoid the mashed potatoes in the cafeteria as if
18   your life depended on it.
19 LISA: Really?
20 SUE: Really. They are deadly. Come on, I'll introduce you to
21   a couple of other kids.
22 LISA: Well, OK. Thanks. *(They exit.)*

2. Party Line

Topic: Gossip between guys on the telephone is accidentally overheard.

Cast:
GEORGE
JOEY
PAUL

1 *(This is a telephone conversation. Actors do not look at each*
2 *other. PAUL is not on the phone at the beginning of the play.*
3 *GEORGE is sitting in a chair facing Stage Left, playing video*
4 *games or using a laptop. JOEY is lying on the floor on the*
5 *opposite side of the stage, leafing through a motorcycle*
6 *magazine.)*
7 **GEORGE: Speak.**
8 **JOEY: Hey.**
9 **GEORGE: Hey.** *(Pause)*
10 **JOEY: Whatcha doin'?**
11 **GEORGE: Nothing. You?**
12 **JOEY: Me neither.** *(Pause)* **You want to three-way call Paul?**
13 **GEORGE: Sure.** *(JOEY pushes some buttons on his phone.*
14 *PAUL enters Upstage and sits between the two boys, but it's*
15 *important that he does not glance at either kid. He walks*
16 *while answering phone.)*
17 **PAUL: Yo.**
18 **JOEY: Yo yourself.**
19 **PAUL: What's up?**
20 **JOEY: Nothin. You?**
21 **PAUL: Nothin. You talked to George lately?**
22 **JOEY: As a matter of fact —**
23 **PAUL: He's such a jerk.** *(GEORGE is surprised and angry by*
24 *hearing this. He is listening even more intently.)*
25 **JOEY: Huh?**

1   PAUL: I'm really mad at him today.

2   JOEY: What? What's wrong?

3   PAUL: I heard that he told Amanda that Betsy said I was a

4   jerk.

5   JOEY: Betsy thinks everyone's a jerk.

6   PAUL: That's not the point.

7   JOEY: Paul, I think you should know —

8   PAUL: I'm not even going to tell him about the party I'm

9   going to have on Saturday.

10 JOEY: Paul —

11 PAUL: No, you can't talk me out of it. He's a jerk and I don't

12   want him at my party.

13 GEORGE: I wouldn't come anyway.

14 PAUL: What? Who's that?

15 GEORGE: It's me, and I didn't tell Amanda. And I don't

16   want to come to your stupid party.

17 PAUL: Joey, why didn't you tell me George was on three-

18   way?

19 JOEY: I tried, but you kept cutting me off and —

20 GEORGE: Anyway, Amanda said she thinks *you're* a jerk.

21 PAUL: She did not.

22 JOEY: Hey, guys —

23 GEORGE: Did too. None of the girls like you because you're

24   such a jerk. *(All three BOYS' bodies should reflect tension*

25   *and anger.)*

26 PAUL: All the girls like me and you're just jealous.

27 GEORGE: *I'm* jealous? You're the one that's jealous. Ever

28   since my dad got that new Jag —

29 PAUL: I couldn't care less about your father's stupid car.

30 GEORGE: Oh, really? I bet —

31 JOEY: *Everybody shut up! (Long pause)* **OK,** everyone

32   breathe. George, Paul, you're best friends. Stop fighting.

33   It's stupid.

34 PAUL: You're stupid.

35 GEORGE: You really are stupid, Joey. Gosh, what a mess

1   this is. And all because of you.
2   PAUL: Yeah, why did you start this fight anyway?
3   JOEY: *Me?* *(Jumps up.)* I didn't start —
4   GEORGE: Hey, Paul, meet me in the private chat room. I
5   don't think I want *him* in on our conversation anymore.
6   *(Hangs up.)*
7   PAUL: Right. Joey, you're a loser. *(Hangs up.)*
8   JOEY: Hello? Anybody there? *(Hangs up.)* Sometimes it just
9   doesn't pay to get out of bed in the morning.

3. Battle of Wits

Topic: A bully and a clever kid match wits.

Cast:

JOE: A bully. He should be tough, sarcastic, and edgy. Costume suggestions would include punk type clothing, chains, and multi-colored hair.

TONY: A smart kid. Smart *and* smart aleck. He's sarcastic and enjoys his superiority. He should be dressed as nerdy as desired, even a pocket protector might work. More appropriate would be modern clothing, perhaps slightly outdated or ill-fitting — pants too short, socks with sandals.

1　*(Scene opens as TONY is sitting in a chair, reading a textbook.*
2　*JOE enters, spots TONY, and saunters over.)*
3　**JOE: What are you doing?**
4　**TONY: Huh?**
5　**JOE: I asked you what you were doing.**
6　**TONY: Uhhhh ... sitting?**
7　**JOE: I can see that. Why are you sitting in my chair?**
8　**TONY: This is your chair?**
9　**JOE: You know it is. What are you doing in it?**
10　**TONY: Well ... I'm sitting in it.**
11　**JOE: Get out.**
12　**TONY:** *(Considers a minute.)* **No thanks.**
13　**JOE: Huh?**
14　**TONY: I'm actually pretty comfortable here, so you go find**
15　　**yourself another chair.**
16　**JOE: You're kidding, right? Don't you know who I am?**
17　**TONY: Sure I know who you are. We had gym together last**
18　　**year, but I think you were in detention more than gym.**
19　**JOE: You got a lot of attitude for a little punk. Think you're**
20　　**pretty bad, don't you?**
21　**TONY: No, actually, I'm very good. I even passed the fourth**

1   grade. How about you?

2 JOE: I'm gonna count and you'd better be up and outta my

3   sight by the time I get to three.

4 TONY: Wait!

5 JOE: Have a change of heart?

6 TONY: No, I just didn't want to watch you strain yourself by

7   trying to count all the way up to three.

8 JOE: You got a smart mouth to go with that attitude. I think

9   I'm going to have to teach you a lesson.

10 TONY: Not possible.

11 JOE: Huh?

12 TONY: I sincerely doubt there is anything you know that you

13   could teach to me.

14 JOE: You wanna bet? I could teach you how to keep your

15   mouth shut and to get out of a person's chair when they

16   tell you to.

17 TONY: My mother tried to tell me to do something once. I'm

18   sure gonna miss her. *(Laughs at his own joke.)*

19 JOE: Huh?

20 TONY: You say that a lot. *Huh?* That's a sound that

21   represents tremendous depth of thought.

22 JOE: I don't know what you're talking about, but I'm getting

23   sick of your mouth. This is your last chance. Get up.

24 TONY: What do you want with this chair, anyway?

25 JOE: I just want to sit.

26 TONY: There's another chair right over there. *(Points to chair*

27   *across stage.)*

28 JOE: *(Without looking)* I don't want that one. I want this one.

29 TONY: Trust me, it's not all that comfortable.

30 JOE: *(Gritting teeth, getting really mad)* Get out of my chair.

31 TONY: I tell you what. I'll go get that other chair and we can

32   sit here and have a nice heart-to-heart talk. OK?

33 JOE: Why would I want to talk to you?

34 TONY: Well, we've been having this great little five-minute

35   conversation and I hate to cut you off, but, if you have

1   to run ... well, I guess I'll see you later.
2 JOE: Huh?
3 TONY: Right. Bye now.
4 JOE: *(A little confused)* **Uhhhh ... OK. Bye.** *(He leaves.)*
5 TONY: *(Shakes his head.)* **Never enter into a battle of wits**
6   **with an unarmed man.** *(Back to reading book)*

4. That's What Buddies are For

Topic: Friends try to gently break bad news to another friend.

Cast:
BOB: a sincere, kind, positive thinker trying to do what is best
TOM: sincere and down-to-earth
MIKE: happy that his friends care about him but a little discouraged by their not being "with the program"

1   *(Scene opens with BOB and TOM standing Center Stage,*
2   *talking in a stage whisper — regular talking made to sound*
3   *like actors are whispering so as not to be overheard, but must*
4   *be loud enough for audience to hear. MIKE is Off-Stage.)*
5   BOB: If you don't tell him, I will.
6   TOM: Sure, I'd love to see that.
7   BOB: I will. I'll tell him. I'm not afraid of him.
8   TOM: You are *so* afraid of him, you'll probably run as soon
9   as you see him coming.
10 BOB: Come on, he's our friend. He's your *best* friend.
11   Wouldn't you want him to tell you if it were the other way
12   around?
13 TOM: Yeah, but I like all my teeth exactly where they are. I
14   really don't want to lose any to his fist.
15 BOB: Oh, grow up, Tom. He's not going to hit you. Look —
16   here he comes. Step up and do the right thing. *(TOM*
17   *cowers behind BOB. MIKE enters casually, crosses to boys at*
18   *Center.)*
19 MIKE: Hey, losers, what's up?
20 TOM: Nothing. Not a thing. Nothing's up, right Bob?
21 BOB: Great going.
22 MIKE: OK, spill it. What's wrong?

1 BOB: *(Obviously nervous, stuttering)* **Wrong? Oh, nothing's**
2   **wrong. I mean, not wrong exactly. A little ...**
3   **uncomfortable. But not really** *wrong.* **You know,** *wrong*
4   **sounds like it's a big deal, and it really isn't. It's only ...**
5 TOM: *(To BOB)* **Would you either shut up or say something**
6   **worthwhile?** *(To MIKE)* **The truth is, Mike, we gotta talk**
7   **to you.**
8 MIKE: **I don't like the way that sounds.**
9 BOB: **Then you're really gonna love what comes next.**
10 TOM: *(Looking angrily at BOB)* **The thing is, Mike ... well ...**
11   *(Turns in a panic to BOB.)* **Tell him, Bob.**
12 BOB: *(Sarcastically)* **Right. Like I'm gonna tell him.**
13 MIKE: *(Amused rather than annoyed)* **One of you better tell**
14   **me or I'll give you something to talk about.**
15 BOB: *Tom* **really wants to tell you. After all,** *he is* **your best**
16   **friend and you'd want to hear this from him.**
17 TOM: *(To BOB, sarcastically)* **Thanks.** *(Turns back to MIKE.*
18   *Gathers up his courage.)* **The thing is, Mike ... well, I don't**
19   **think Judy is going to be able to go to the dance with**
20   **you Saturday.**
21 MIKE: *(Without expression)* **You don't, huh?**
22 TOM: *(Very nervously)* **No. The truth is ... well, what I mean**
23   **to say, is ...**
24 BOB: *(Blurts it out.)* **She's going with Spencer Thompson.**
25 MIKE: *(Still without much expression)* **Spencer Thompson?**
26 TOM: **Yeah, I heard him talking to some guys in the locker**
27   **room and he said he's taking Judy to the dance. I'm**
28   **really sorry, Mike.**
29 BOB: **Yeah, she's a sneaky one, that Judy. I always said you**
30   **couldn't trust her. Never trust a beautiful girl, that's my**
31   **motto.**
32 TOM: *(Trying to get MIKE's spirits up)* **Yeah, you can do better**
33   **than her anyway, Mike. I mean, she's pretty and all, but**
34   **she's not all that and a bag of chips.**
35 BOB: **Yeah, she thinks she's so terrific with all that**

1   cheerleading and blonde, beautiful hair and that BMW ...
2 MIKE: *(Still not letting on to his feelings)* **I guess I should be**
3   **upset, huh?**
4 TOM: *(Cowers behind BOB again.)* **If you want to hit someone,**
5   **I'm sure Bob would be happy to accommodate you.**
6 MIKE: *(Smugly)* **Actually, I dumped Judy last Tuesday. I'm**
7   **taking Marlene Talbot to the dance.**
8 BOB: *(A little embarrassed)* **Marlene Talbot? The other**
9   **cheerleader?**
10 TOM: *(Also embarrassed)* **Also with the long, blonde beautiful**
11   **hair?**
12 MIKE: *(Happy to see them uncomfortable)* **Yeah, I see you know**
13   **her.**
14 TOM: **Gosh, you do like a certain type, don't you?**
15 BOB: **Tell me something, Mike.**
16 MIKE: **Yeah?**
17 TOM: **How's a guy like ... well, like *you* get two gorgeous**
18   **girls like that to go out with you?**
19 MIKE: **It must be my good looks and charming personality.**
20 BOB: *(Sarcastic, befuddled)* **That must be it.**

5. Bermuda

Topic: Miscommunication among friends.

Cast:
BRITTANY: easy-going, sincere, and an honest friend
INEZ: a drama queen and not against using manipulation to get what she wants
AMELIA: a straight-shooter and has no idea what all the fuss is about

1 *(Scene opens with BRITTANY sitting alone, Center Stage,*
2 *moping, obviously angry and upset. INEZ enters.)*
3 **INEZ:** Hey, Brittany, what's up?
4 **BRITTANY:** *(Snappy)* Don't talk to me. I'm in a bad mood.
5 **INEZ:** Aw, I'm sorry. What's wrong?
6 **BRITTANY:** Didn't I tell you not to talk to me?
7 **INEZ:** Gosh, you *are* in a bad mood. C'mon, you gotta talk
8 about it. Tell me. *(Sits next to her.)*
9 **BRITTANY:** Oh, all right. Can you keep a secret?
10 **INEZ:** *(Excited at the prospect of gossip)* Me? Oh, sure, yes, of
11 course! I can keep a secret forever. I'll *never* tell anyone.
12 Tell me, tell me, tell me!
13 **BRITTANY:** I heard Amelia is moving to Bermuda.
14 **INEZ:** *(Shocked)* What?
15 **BRITTANY:** Like, next week! And she didn't tell anyone! I'm
16 pretty mad at her for not telling us.
17 **INEZ:** *(Progressively louder and more shocked)* Bermuda?
18 Really?
19 **BRITTANY:** We won't have time to organize a party, or even
20 to buy her a gift. I can't imagine why she didn't tell
21 anyone.
22 **INEZ:** *(Lost in her own thoughts)* Bermuda?
23 **BRITTANY:** *(Irritated)* Yes! Bermuda! Would you try to focus,
24 please?
25 **INEZ:** *(Dreamily)* I've always wanted to go to Bermuda.

1 BRITTANY: You're helping a lot. What about Amelia?

2 INEZ: *(Still without a clue)* Yeah, I'm sure her mom would let

3   me stay with them if I came to visit. I could come during

4   Christmas break. I heard it's really beautiful and warm

5   in Bermuda in the winter.

6 BRITTANY: *(Yelling in frustration)* **Inez!**

7 INEZ: *(Coming back to the present)* **Um ... what?**

8 BRITTANY: You're not even thinking about Amelia. We're

9   going to miss her so much! We've been friends forever!

10   I'm still pretty mad she — uh oh, here she comes.

11   *(AMELIA innocently enters from opposite side from which*

12   *INEZ entered.)*

13 INEZ: *(Very sweetly)* **Hello, dear, dear friend Amelia.**

14 AMELIA: *(Put off by INEZ's friendliness)* **Uh ... hi?**

15 BRITTANY: I'm so mad at you, Amelia!

16 AMELIA: *(Really put off by BRITTANY's anger)* **Me? What did I**

17   **do this time?**

18 INEZ: *(Still as sweet as pie)* **Don't pay any attention to her,**

19   **good buddy. I'm still your very close, very good friend,**

20   **right?**

21 AMELIA: *(To BRITTANY)* **Since when is she my very good**

22   **friend?**

23 BRITTANY: *(Disgusted and still angry)* **Since she found out**

24   **you're moving to a beautiful island! And I'm very angry**

25   **that you didn't tell us.**

26 INEZ: *(Still sweetly)* **Don't worry about Brittany, Amelia.**

27   **She's just not as understanding as I am, your very good**

28   **friend.**

29 AMELIA: *(Matter-of-factly)* **I'm not moving to any island.**

30 INEZ: Oh. I thought Bermuda was an island. Oh, well, I do

31   know it's beautiful.

32 AMELIA: I'm not moving to Bermuda.

33 INEZ and BRITTANY: *(Shocked)* **What?**

34 BRITTANY: Tom told me —

35 AMELIA: *(Suddenly understands what the confusion is about.)*

1   Oh, he was talking about our social studies project.
2   We're supposed to get a map and pick a place we would
3   like to move to and map out the time and —
4 INEZ: *(No longer sweetly)* You're *not* moving to Bermuda?!
5 AMELIA: Uh, no. Don't you think I would have said
6   something?
7 BRITTANY: *(Authentically cheerful)* Oh, I'm so glad! I was so
8   upset that you were moving and hadn't told us.
9 AMELIA: *(Truly touched by this)* That's really nice, Brittany.
10   *(To INEZ)* Were you worried too, Inez?
11 INEZ: *(She had been getting more and more upset. Finally blurts*
12   *out)* Don't talk to me, you jerk! Now who am I going to
13   visit over Christmas break? *(She storms off.)*
14 AMELIA: *(Completely confused by the change in INEZ's*
15   *behavior)* Huh?
16 BRITTANY: Don't worry about her, Amelia. At least you
17   know who your *real* friends are!

6. Funny Isn't Always Funny

Topic: A play on gossiping.

Cast:
GINGER: trying to do the right thing, even if it's uncomfortable
CRYSTAL: unaware of how innocent comments can be hurtful

1   *(Scene opens with CRYSTAL walking across the stage and*
2   *GINGER running to catch up with her.)*
3 GINGER: Hey, Crystal, that was really not cool. *(They stop.)*
4 CRYSTAL: *(Innocently confused, she doesn't understand.)*
5   What?
6 GINGER: What you said back there to Quinn.
7 CRYSTAL: *(Still confused)* What are you talking about?
8 GINGER: *(Not too accusing, more said out of concern.*
9   *Cautiously)* I heard you when I was walking past the
10   cafeteria. You were laughing at her haircut.
11 CRYSTAL: *(Trying to brush it off)* It was just a joke. Everyone
12   was laughing.
13 GINGER: Quinn wasn't.
14 CRYSTAL: *(Not angry yet, almost amused)* Who are you, like
15   the moral police?
16 GINGER: *(Pauses. Comes to a decision.)* I guess I am. I mean,
17   I don't like to see people getting hurt.
18 CRYSTAL: She wasn't hurt. It was just a joke.
19 GINGER: Jokes can really hurt. Even if you aren't trying to
20   be mean, it can still be really hurtful for people to point
21   out the things about you that are different or odd.
22 CRYSTAL: *(Giggling)* Well, her haircut is sure both different
23   *and* odd. She looks like a cross between Clay Aiken and
24   Sponge Bob.

1   GINGER: *(Angry at her joking)* **That's just what I'm talking**
2   **about. Stop saying things like that about her hair.**
3   CRYSTAL: Gosh, Ginger, this is just what friends do. Don't
4   you ever tease your friends?
5   GINGER: I do sometimes, but then someone teased me
6   once about something and it really hurt my feelings.
7   CRYSTAL: When was that?
8   GINGER: *(Crosses in front of CRYSTAL during this monologue,*
9   *but doesn't look at her.)* **My dad had lost his job and we**
10   had to move into a really small apartment. We couldn't
11   really afford to buy new clothes, so we bought some
12   shoes that I found at the Salvation Army. They were
13   really cool and I liked them a lot. They would have been
14   like seventy-five dollars in a regular store and I only paid
15   like three dollars for them. When I went to this new
16   school, some kid said something about me having the
17   ugliest shoes in the school. I guess she was trying to be
18   friendly or something, but I was so embarrassed I
19   wanted to hide in the bathroom all day.
20 CRYSTAL: *(Not really believing this would upset GINGER)* **Did**
21   **that really hurt your feelings?**
22 GINGER: *(Trying to make her understand)* **Yeah. I mean, we**
23   really couldn't afford nice shoes and I was really
24   embarrassed. I thought my shoes were cool, but I guess
25   they really weren't. Hasn't anyone ever made fun of you
26   and that made you feel bad?
27 CRYSTAL: *(Pause)* **Well, yeah, I guess. My great-aunt sent**
28   me a handmade shirt from a Navajo reservation and I
29   wore it to school one day. The girls called me
30   Pocahontas for a week.
31 GINGER: How did that make you feel?
32 CRYSTAL: Pretty lousy.
33 GINGER: Exactly. Even when people are just trying to be
34   funny, the things they say can really hurt.
35 CRYSTAL: *(Beginning to understand)* **I guess you're right. I**

1   shouldn't have called Quinn Lassie. I guess I'll go

2   apologize.

3   GINGER: That's a good idea. I think the best thing you can

4   do is stop listening to other people joking and making

5   fun of people and remind them how it might feel to be on

6   the receiving end of that kind of "joke."

7   CRYSTAL: Good point. Come with me?

8   GINGER: Sure. *(They exit.)*

7. Out of the Line of Vision

Topic: A play concerning judgments based on appearance.

Cast:
CHRIS: tries to be open-minded and fair
TAYLOR: judgmental and easily frightened by the unknown
DIRTY MAN: poorly dressed, dirty, and looks homeless
FANCY MAN: the opposite of Dirty Man — well-dressed, etc.

1   *(Scene works with CHRIS and TAYLOR walking across the*
2   *stage.)*
3   **CHRIS:** *(Excited)* I can't wait to see this play. It's supposed
4   to be really good.
5   **TAYLOR:** *(Nervously looking around)* Yeah, but I hate being
6   downtown. It's so gross.
7   **CHRIS:** Well, at least the light rail let us off like one block
8   from the theatre. Let's just walk fast.
9   **DIRTY MAN:** *(Approaches BOYS cautiously, hat in hand.)*
10   'Scuse me, kids. Can you spare a quarter?
11   **TAYLOR:** *(Frightened and disgusted, grabs CHRIS's arm.)* Ew,
12   Chris, don't look at him.
13   **CHRIS:** *(To TAYLOR, confused)* Huh?
14   **TAYLOR:** That guy. He's dirty. He's probably homeless. Just
15   ignore him. They can be really nasty. Let's walk faster.
16   **DIRTY MAN:** *(Kindly, not disturbed by the rejection)* You two
17   kids have a blessed day now. *(He walks Off-Stage.)*
18   **CHRIS:** Did you hear that? He said "blessed." Now I feel bad
19   that we ignored him.
20   **TAYLOR:** Just because he said "blessed" doesn't mean he's
21   religious or anything. He probably thinks that makes
22   people feel more sorry for him.

1   **FANCY MAN:** *(Enters from opposite entrance from where DIRTY*
2   *MAN exited. Appears sincere and a little too friendly.)* **Hello,**
3   **children. Can you give me directions to the Rigley**
4   **Theatre?**
5   **TAYLOR: Oh, sure. I think if you go up to that traffic light**
6   **and turn right, it's right on that block.**
7   **FANCY MAN: Gee, I don't think I can find it on my own.**
8   **Would you mind walking with me?**
9   **TAYLOR:** *(Kindly, without hesitation)* **Sure. It's not too far out**
10   **of our way.**
11   **CHRIS:** *(Pulls on TAYLOR's sleeve, speaks in a stage whisper)*
12   **Taylor! You shouldn't go with a stranger. We don't know**
13   **him!**
14   **TAYLOR: Oh, ease up, Chris. Look how nicely he's dressed.**
15   **He's OK. We really should be polite to people.**
16   **CHRIS: Like you were to that homeless guy?**
17   **TAYLOR: That's different. We're not supposed to be nice to**
18   **gross people, only clean people.**
19   **CHRIS: Where did you get that idea? Be kind to well-dressed**
20   **people and ridicule and ignore those dirty people.**
21   **TAYLOR: Don't be sarcastic. This guy is perfectly fine and**
22   **you're just being bullheaded.**
23   **FANCY MAN: You know,** *(Mimes getting into a car)* **I hurt my**
24   **foot last week and I really can't walk very far. Would you**
25   **mind very much getting in my car and helping me find**
26   **that bank?**
27   **CHRIS:** *(Now highly suspicious)* **I thought you said you**
28   **wanted Rigley Theatre?**
29   **FANCY MAN: Oh, uh, right. That's where I'm going. I'm so**
30   **absentminded.**
31   **TAYLOR:** *(Also finally understanding the possible danger)* **Uh, I**
32   **don't think we should get into your car.**
33   **FANCY MAN:** *(Trying to be persuasive, beginning to sound odd)*
34   **Oh, come on. It's only a block or two, like you said.**
35   **You'd really be helping me. I'm supposed to meet my**

1   grandmother and I don't want to be late.
2   TAYLOR: *(Wanting to believe)* Oh, if your grandmother is
3   there, I'm sure it's OK.
4   CHRIS: Taylor! *(To FANCY MAN)* Uh, sorry Mister, but we've
5   got to get going. We can't go with you.
6   FANCY MAN: *(Not nice at all now. Firm and angry)* Come on,
7   now, don't be difficult. You said you would help.
8   CHRIS: We've really got to get going.
9   FANCY MAN: *(Very angry and ominous)* Get into the car.
10   Now.
11 DIRTY MAN: *(Running on from Off-Stage)* Hey, kids, I was
12   wondering where you were. You really shouldn't have run
13   off like that. I've been looking for you.
14 TAYLOR: *(Confused but beginning to understand)* Oh ... uh ...
15   sorry, uh ... Uncle Bob. We were just trying to give this
16   man some directions.
17 DIRTY MAN: *(To FANCY MAN)* Sorry, fella, but I've got to get
18   these kids back home before their mom sends a search
19   committee out for me. You ready, kids?
20 CHRIS: Oh, sure. *(To TAYLOR, forcefully)* Let's go. *(FANCY*
21   *MAN drives off angry. ALL watch him go.)*
22 TAYLOR: *(To DIRTY MAN)* Thank you, Mister. He was weird.
23   I think he was —
24 DIRTY MAN: No problem. I thought he looked like he was
25   looking for trouble. I'm glad you're OK. You know, you
26   should never get into a car with a stranger. I'm sure your
27   mother told you that.
28 CHRIS: Uh, yes, of course. It's just that he looked so ...
29 TAYLOR: Nice.
30 DIRTY MAN: Well, looks can be deceiving, can't they? *(Gives*
31   *them a minute to consider.)*
32 TAYLOR: *(Looking at DIRTY MAN, pauses, and recognizes his*
33   *mistake.)* Yes, you're absolutely right. Thanks so much
34   for coming to our rescue. *(Gives him some change.)*
35 DIRTY MAN: Don't mention it. God bless you two. You'd

1   better get going. Be careful now.
2 CHRIS: We will. Thank you. Really, thanks so much. And I'm
3   sorry for —
4 DIRTY MAN: Don't mention it. Really, don't mention it. Bye.
5   *(He leaves.)*
6 TAYLOR: Well, we completely misjudged those two men,
7   didn't we?
8 CHRIS: Yeah, and all because of what they looked like. Who
9   would have thought?
10 TAYLOR: I guess that shows that you really can't judge
11   people by how they look. Are we going to make our show
12   on time?
13 CHRIS: Oh, yeah, but we'd better hurry. I can't wait to see
14   Julie Quinn.
15 TAYLOR: Oh? Have you seen her act before?
16 CHRIS: No, but she's gorgeous. If she was a dinosaur, she'd
17   be a babe-a-saurus.
18 TAYLOR: So much for your lesson on judging books by their
19   cover.
20 CHRIS: Oh, was this play a book first?
21 TAYLOR: Let's go. I think you need to get out of the sun.

8. The Project

Topic: Group of students trying to get motivated to put together a project

Cast:
COURTNEY: a go-getter, trying to work correctly and up against lazy classmates
BEN: would rather be anywhere but here; he's lazy, sarcastic, and bored
ILAN: the class brainiac and extremely well-spoken
KIM: nice, fun-loving, and loves to eat

1   *(ALL sitting around in various positions. COURTNEY has*
2   *paper and pencil, trying to take notes. BEN is trying to sleep.*
3   *ILAN is sitting upright, hyper-focused. KIM is playing with her*
4   *hair, her mind obviously elsewhere.)*
5 **COURTNEY:** *(Obviously been working at this for a while)* **If we**
6   **don't start on this, we're never gonna finish.**
7 **BEN:** *(Tossing a ball in the air and catching it)* **I hate these**
8   **stupid projects. Why do we have to do this stuff**
9   **anyway?**
10 **ILAN:** *(Softly, but assuredly and clearly)* **To enhance our**
11   **learning and increase our appreciation for the world**
12   **around us.**
13 **KIM: You sound like a walking encyclopedia, Ilan.**
14 **ILAN: Well, I think it's an interesting and engaging**
15   **opportunity.**
16 **BEN: Of course you do. You're like a miniature teacher.**
17 **COURTNEY:** *(Clapping hands)* **People! People! No bickering!**
18   **We're gonna have to** *start* **if we ever want to** *finish.*
19 **KIM:** *(Shifts weight, looks at her nails.)* **Isn't it time to take a**
20   **break? I think I need a snack.**
21 **COURTNEY: We just started! No breaks. Let's at least get**
22   **started.**

1 ILAN: I think we should explore all the possible
2   manifestations of precipitation in order to determine the
3   appropriate methodology of commencing our project.
4 BEN: Is he even speaking English?
5 KIM: No English I ever heard.
6 COURTNEY: I think he said we should think about the
7   different kinds of rain in order to figure out how to start.
8 BEN: Why didn't he just say that?
9 ILAN: I did.
10 BEN: *(Sits up.)* No, this is what you said: "Blah blah blah.
11   Blah blah blah. Blah blah blah project."
12 COURTNEY: You're not helping matters, Ben. We *have* to
13   get started.
14 KIM: *(Whining)* I'm hungry.
15 BEN: *(To ILAN and KIM)* Ryan had a huge brownie for lunch
16   today. He wouldn't share, but it looked really good.
17 KIM: Did it have chocolate chips?
18 BEN: I think so. But no nuts. I hate nuts.
19 KIM: Me, too. My mom puts nuts in her cookies every
20   Christmas and I won't eat them.
21 ILAN: Oftentimes an underlying allergic sensitivity to nuts
22   and legumes of all types causes gastrointestinal upset
23   and is mistaken for disliking when it may actually
24   represent an allergy.
25 BEN and KIM: *(Pause, then say together)* *Huh?*
26 COURTNEY: *(Exasperated. Throws pencil in the air and drops*
27   *notebook.)* I give up! I'm writing this for our paper,
28   *Sometimes it rains. Sometimes it snows. Sometimes it's*
29   *foggy. The end.* How's that?
30 BEN: I *love* it.
31 KIM: Me, too. You hand that in, Courtney. Come on, Ben,
32   let's hit the vending machines. *(BEN and KIM leave.*
33   *There's a pause.)*
34 COURTNEY: I was kidding.
35 ILAN: *(Pause)* Do you oftentimes sense that you are alone in

1   the universe without an understanding soul existing on
2   this whole planet?
3   **COURTNEY:** *(Looks at him like he's crazy.)* **All the time.**

9. Gossip

Topic: A play that shows the hurtful side of gossip.

Cast:
SASHA, BRIANNA, and KIM: typical girls — chatty, gossipy, and enjoying their newfound common target
COURTNEY: trying to bring some decency to the other girls

1   *(SASHA, BRIANNA, and KIM gather Center Stage. They are*
2   *carrying school books, dressed trendy, and giggling.)*
3   **SASHA: Did you *see* what she was wearing?**
4   **BRIANNA: Oh, good grief, does she even own a mirror?**
5   **KIM: I think I saw shoes like hers at the Salvation Army!**
6   *(COURNTEY enters and joins the group, smiling at her*
7   *friends.)*
8   **COURTNEY: What are you guys talking about?**
9   **BRIANNA:** *(Happy to share the gossip)* **Oh, Courtney, you**
10   **should have seen what Lisa was wearing at the mall last**
11   **night.**
12 **SASHA: It was this bright blue shirt ...** *(Starts laughing.)*
13 **BRIANNA: And those pants ...** *(Laughs.)*
14 **KIM: No, the best part was the shoes.** *(All but COURTNEY*
15   *laugh.)*
16 **COURTNEY:** *(Confused and disturbed)* **You're making fun of**
17   **Lisa?**
18 **SASHA:** *(Dismissively)* **No, we're not making fun of her.**
19 **BRIANNA:** *(Still giggling a little)* **It's just that she was**
20   **wearing this really funny outfit.**
21 **COURTNEY: That *is* making fun of her.**
22 **KIM: Come on, Courtney, it was really funny.**
23 **BRIANNA: If you had seen it, you'd be laughing too.**
24 **COURTNEY:** *(Trying to make her point understood)* **It's mean**
25   **to make fun of people.**
26 **BRIANNA: Oh, come on, you do it too.**

1 COURTNEY: No, I don't.
2 SASHA: We don't mean anything mean by it. I like Lisa a
3   lot.
4 KIM: Yeah. She's one of our best friends.
5 BRIANNA: If only she knew how to dress! *(All but COURTNEY*
6   *laugh.)*
7 COURTNEY: *(Getting angry now)* You guys, it's really not
8   nice to make fun of other people. Maybe she can't afford
9   nice clothes like you.
10 BRIANNA: In her case, it's not about money. It's about
11   taste!
12 KIM: It doesn't cost anything to match colors!
13 COURTNEY: That's not the point. It's still mean.
14 SASHA: *(Possibly understanding, still smiling)* You're probably
15   right. But it *was* funny.
16 KIM: *(Getting a little more serious)* Maybe you're right,
17   Courtney. We are sometimes mean to each other.
18 BRIANNA: Right. Remember how you felt, Sasha, when you
19   got that new haircut last year and all the boys laughed
20   at you?
21 SASHA: *(No longer smiling and remembering with pain)* Oh,
22   don't remind me. I almost didn't come to school. I cried
23   every night for a week.
24 COURTNEY: See? Even when people are kidding it can be
25   really hurtful.
26 SASHA: Yeah, maybe you're right. It really did hurt my
27   feelings.
28 KIM: We don't mean to be mean to each other. Sometimes
29   we just think things are funny.
30 COURTNEY: Well, whether you mean it or not isn't the
31   point. You can really hurt someone's feelings even
32   without meaning to.
33 BRIANNA: I guess we should all work on this, huh?
34 SASHA: That's a good idea. Let's make a pact to try to stop
35   each other from making fun of other kids.

1   BRIANNA: That sounds like fun. We can be like judges.
2   Whoever makes the fewest amount of slip ups gets a
3   quarter from the rest of us at the end of the week.
4   COURTNEY: Count me in!
5   SASHA: I just hope I don't go broke trying to get rid of the
6   habit!
7   BRIANNA: Now we'd better all go talk to Lisa.
8   SASHA: Let's go!

10. The Sweater

Topic: A funny skit about the dynamics between girlfriends.

Cast:
BRENDA: sly, not really honest, and trying to influence Marilyn for her own purposes
MARYLYN: innocent, kind, and a good friend who listens to Brenda's advice

1 *(The GIRLS are standing in front of a mirror. MARILYN has on*
2 *a sweater — any color but red. Both GIRLS are evaluating. An*
3 *option would be to have a table of sweaters with MARILYN*
4 *holding up a particular sweater instead of wearing one.)*
5 BRENDA: *(Considering it)* **I don't think you should buy it.**
6 MARILYN: *(Turning this way and that, checking out the sweater*
7 *from all angles)* **Why not? It's fabulous.**
8 BRENDA: **Why not? Let's see.** *(Counts on fingers.)* **It's ugly,**
9 **doesn't fit you, and it costs a million dollars.**
10 MARILYN: **It is not. I love it.**
11 BRENDA: *(Throws hands up in the air, as if in surrender.)* **Fine.**
12 **Buy it. But don't count on me to stick up for you when**
13 **your parents yell at you for paying too much for a**
14 **sweater or when the kids at school make fun of you.**
15 MARILYN: *(Beginning to show some doubt, looking a little less*
16 *pleased with the view in the mirror)* **Wow, you're really**
17 **being mean. There's nothing wrong with this sweater.**
18 **It's pretty.**
19 BRENDA: *(Shrugging)* **If you say so.**
20 MARILYN: **I don't get you. You're the one who picked it out**
21 **for me to try on.**
22 BRENDA: **Well, I didn't look at the price. And I couldn't**
23 **really see how ugly it was until you put it on.**
24 MARILYN: **But it's your favorite color.**
25 BRENDA: *(Defensively)* **I like red now.**

1   MARILYN: And didn't you buy a sweater for five dollars more
2   last week?
3   BRENDA: It was on sale.
4   MARILYN: *(Closely examining it)* I don't know. I think it's
5   really pretty.
6   BRENDA: Well, good luck. Good luck ruining your fashion
7   reputation in front the entire middle school tomorrow
8   when you wear that hideous sweater.
9   MARILYN: *(Looking carefully in the mirror)* You really think it's
10   that bad?
11 BRENDA: Trust me, Marilyn. Buying that sweater would be
12   the worst mistake you make this year.
13 MARILYN: Well, OK. If you really think so. *(Goes Off-Stage to*
14   *change out of sweater, or just replaces it if she doesn't have*
15   *it on).*
16 BRENDA: *(Shouting Off-Stage, if MARILYN is Off-Stage, smiling*
17   *to herself)* I do. You won't be sorry you didn't buy it. Let's
18   go to Macy's and see what they have.
19 MARILYN: *(Coming back On-Stage)* All right. I'm gonna stop
20   for a soda.
21 BRENDA: OK, I'll meet you. I want to call my mom.
22 MARILYN: OK. *(Exits.)*
23 BRENDA: *(Waits until MARILYN is gone and picks up the same*
24   *sweater.)* This is gonna look *great* on me!

11. Student Council

Topic: A play about compromise and working together in times of conflict as two boys negotiate a run for student council.

Cast:
MIGUEL: typical smart kid, average looking, and highly intelligent
JAKE: a babe magnet and more into popularity and girls than politics

1   *(JAKE joins MIGUEL at the cafeteria table.)*
2   JAKE: Hey.
3   MIGUEL: *(Cautiously friendly)* **Hey.**
4   JAKE: **So I hear you put your name in for student council**
5   **president.**
6   MIGUEL: **Yeah. You too?**
7   JAKE: **Yeah.** *(Pause. Continues somewhat arrogantly.)* **You**
8   **know, you might as well give it up. We both know I'll win**
9   **in, like, a landslide.**
10   MIGUEL: **Not necessarily. Since sixty percent of the school**
11   **is male, I think my chances are good.**
12   JAKE: **You mean only girls would vote for me?**
13   MIGUEL: **That's the general consensus.**
14   JAKE: *(Very full of himself)* **You're just jealous because all**
15   **the girls like me.**
16   MIGUEL: **Well, enjoy your popularity, because I'm going to**
17   **be the next student council president.**
18   JAKE: **Why in the world do you think you would beat me in**
19   **the election?**
20   MIGUEL: **Well, let's see. I'm smart. How's that for a start?**
21   JAKE: **You saying I'm not smart?**
22   MIGUEL: *(Sarcastic)* **Oh, no, I would never say that. Quick,**
23   **what's four plus four?**
24   JAKE: *(Dryly)* **Oh, you're a barrel of laughs. I'll have you**
25   **know that there's more to leadership than brains.**

1   MIGUEL: In your case, I would certainly hope so.

2   JAKE: How about personality? Good looks?

3   MIGUEL: Yes, I can see how those qualities would greatly
4   impact the decision-making process concerning school
5   policy.

6   JAKE: *(Still pretty self-assured)* Maybe not, but they will get
7   me elected.

8   MIGUEL: Hmmmm. *(Considers.)* You know who would be the
9   perfect candidate for school council president?

10 JAKE: Napoleon Dynamite?

11 MIGUEL: No, *us.* I mean, us together. My brains and your ...
12   what did you call it? Good looks and personality.

13 JAKE: *(Suspiciously)* You're not talking about some cloning
14   thing, are you?

15 MIGUEL: *(Frustrated)* No, dimwit, I'm talking about
16   teamwork.

17 JAKE: You mean like, working together?

18 MIGUEL: Yeah. I think there are a lot of good changes I could
19   make around the school. I have lots of ideas about
20   fundraising, clubs, school spirit, and new cafeteria
21   menus.

22 JAKE: *(Considering)* I haven't thought about any of those
23   things.

24 MIGUEL: What a surprise. Anyway, I know you're right about
25   one thing. The popular kids do always get elected. What
26   do you say we make a deal?

27 JAKE: Does it involve money?

28 MIGUEL: No. Let's run together. My brains and your looks.
29   President and Vice President. We could both get elected
30   *and* make lots of good changes.

31 JAKE: Who gets to be president?

32 MIGUEL: Does it really matter?

33 JAKE: Not if I get to be president.

34 MIGUEL: Fine. Whatever.

35 JAKE: You're right. We'll make a great team. I like the way

1   you think.
2   MIGUEL: Naturally.
3   JAKE: So you think I'm good-looking, too?
4   MIGUEL: No, but I think other people think so.
5   JAKE: Huh?
6   MIGUEL: Maybe you'd better let me do the talking during
7   the campaign.
8   JAKE: Good idea. I'll work on our theme music.
9   MIGUEL: Perfect.

12. Cooperation

Topic: A skit about diverse personalities trying to work together.

Cast:
MIGUEL: serious, the leader
QUINCY: bored and lazy
WILL: comic relief

1   *(All three GUYS are sitting on the floor. They are surrounded*
2   *by maps, textbooks, notebooks, pens, and anything that*
3   *looks like it might be related to Civil War research.)*
4   MIGUEL: Guys, we are *never* gonna get this thing done.
5   QUINCY: It's stupid. I don't care if we never get done. I
6   don't want to do it.
7   WILL: Did you ever notice how when Brad laughs when he's
8   drinking milk it comes out of his nose?
9   MIGUEL: No, I never noticed and why aren't you working on
10   this project?
11   QUINCY: Because it's stupid and we don't want to do it.
12   MIGUEL: I don't think that's one of the choices Mrs. Davis
13   gave us, Quincy.
14   WILL: It should have been. Choice D: Do *not* do any project
15   on the Civil War, go home, play video games for four
16   hours, and then report your scores to the class
17   tomorrow. Now *that's* a project I could get into.
18   QUINCY: Do we have a half day Friday?
19   MIGUEL: Can we at least see what we have so far?
20   QUINCY: OK, I'll read my paper. "Do you think we have a
21   half day on Friday?"
22   WILL: *(Laughing)* That's more than I have!
23   MIGUEL: I give up! She could have put me with Shannon or
24   Mike, but *no!* I end up with Dumb and Dumber here.
25   QUINCY: Yeah, but which one is Dumber?

1   **QUINCY and WILL:** *(Pause. Point to each other and yell.)* **You**
2   **are!**
3   **MIGUEL:** *(Almost to himself)* **Is murder still against the law in**
4   **this state?**
5   **WILL:** I loved that movie. Jim Carey is so weird!
6   **QUINCY:** Did you see the sequel? It wasn't as good as the
7   first one but it was still funny.
8   **MIGUEL:** Dear Diary: Today I killed two of my classmates
9   and now I will spend the rest of my years in prison ...
10 **WILL:** You know, guys, we really should stop fooling around
11   and get to work on this.
12 **QUINCY:** Yeah, Miguel, quit goofing off and get down to
13   work.
14 **MIGUEL:** *I want my mommy!*

13. Belatedly

Topic: Friends forget another friend's birthday.

Cast:
TANYA and AHMED: good-hearted, but absentminded friends
TOMMY: no clue as to his friends' confusion

1   *(Scene opens with TANYA and AHMED Center Stage, deep in*
2   *conversation.)*
3   **TANYA:** *(Obviously disturbed)* I *completely* forgot it was
4   today.
5   **AHMED:** *(Also upset)* I thought it was in May.
6   **TANYA:** No, September! Remember last year he had that
7   big party right after school started? September
8   sixteenth.
9   **AHMED:** He's gonna be mad at us.
10   **TANYA:** I never forget a birthday. I can't believe I didn't have
11   this written down.
12   **AHMED:** Isn't Cindy supposed to remind everybody?
13   **TANYA:** I know! She's always real good about reminding
14   everyone about birthdays. She really dropped the ball on
15   this one.
16   **AHMED:** What are we gonna do?
17   **TANYA:** I guess the damage is done now. He knows we
18   forgot because we always celebrate first thing in the
19   morning. I don't think there is anything we can do
20   except apologize.
21   **AHMED:** Oh, great. That should be fun. *(Spots TOMMY Off-*
22   *Stage.)* Uh oh, here he comes.
23   **AHMED and TANYA:** *(Count to three silently and then yell as*
24   *TOMMY enters.)* Happy birthday!
25   **TOMMY:** Huh?
26   **TANYA:** *(Overly cheerful, in a false way)* I bet you thought we

1   forgot, didn't you?

2   AHMED: *(Also eagerly cheerful)* **Man, we didn't forget, did we,**
3   **Tanya?**

4   TANYA: No, no of course not.

5   TOMMY: *(Beginning to catch on. Suspiciously)* **Hold on you**
6   **guys, wait a minute. You forgot my birthday?**

7   AHMED: Didn't we just say we didn't?

8   TOMMY: No one said anything during homeroom.

9   TANYA: *(Hesitantly, like she's making it up.)* **Uh, we ... were...**
10   we wanted to surprise you later!

11   TOMMY: Like now?

12   AHMED: Sure, now's a good time!

13   TOMMY: So where's my stuff? The balloons and presents?

14   AHMED: Oh, well ... they're coming a little later.

15   TANYA: We had a little ... problem getting them this
16   morning. But we'll have them later!

17   TOMMY: You guys are a wreck. My birthday is May eighth.
18   *(Smiles.)* **But it was fun to watch you get all riled up and**
19   try to lie your way out of it.

20   TANYA: That's so cruel!

21   AHMED: Yeah, that was mean, Tommy. I wouldn't *really*
22   forget your birthday.

23   TOMMY: Oh yeah? Then how come you forgot it *last* year?

14. Waiting Room

Topic: An adventure in the dentist's waiting room.

Cast:
AHMED: reasonable, smart, easygoing
QUINCY: nice, but with a questionable past
TOMMY: impatient and edgy
MIGUEL: overreacts, highly dramatic, glass-is-half-empty kind of guy, a Mama's boy
DAVEY: calm, reasonable, and laid-back

1   *(ALL are sitting in chairs. Some are looking at magazines.*
2   *They obviously do not know each other.)*
3 **AHMED:** *(Checks his watch, sighs deeply.)* **Does it seem to**
4   **you guys like we've been waiting forever?**
5 **QUINCY: I don't think they've called anyone back there for**
6   **a long time.**
7 **TOMMY:** *(Also checks his watch, fidgets.)* **I really do have**
8   **other places to be. This is taking too long.**
9 **MIGUEL:** *(Growing nervous, clearly easily agitated)* **Do you**
10   **think maybe they all died back there? Maybe a terrorist**
11   **came in the back way and shot everyone. I think that**
12   **would mean that we should all leave, for our own safety.**
13 **DAVEY:** *(Trying to calm down the group)* **You've got quite an**
14   **imagination, dude. We really haven't been here all that long.**
15 **QUINCY:** *(Bored)* **It seems like two hours.**
16 **TOMMY: I've been here longer than all of you. My**
17   **appointment was at two.**
18 **AHMED: Wait a minute. *My* appointment was at two.**
19 **MIGUEL: My appointment wasn't until two.**
20 **DAVEY:** *(Suddenly realizing a problem)* **Hold on. We all have**
21   **appointments scheduled at the same time?**
22 **QUINCY: That can't be right. Maybe there's more than one**
23   **dentist.**

1 ALL: Doctor Davis?

2 AHMED: *(Disgusted)* Nope, only one dentist.

3 MIGUEL: *(A little irritated)* That's the dumbest thing I ever
4   heard. How can we all see the same dentist at the same
5   time?

6 TOMMY: *(Getting up)* Well, you can have my appointment
7   time. I'm outta here.

8 QUINCY: *(Trying to be practical)* I don't think anyone should
9   leave until we at least talk to the receptionist.

10 MIGUEL: I told you, they're all dead in the back.

11 DAVEY: *(Starting to get spooked)* Quit saying that, will ya?

12 MIGUEL: Why? It's true. We should call the police or
13   something.

14 QUINCY: *(Tough guy)* I'm not calling any police. I don't need
15   to have the cops on me again.

16 AHMED: *(Exasperated)* Terrific. Sitting in the dentist's office
17   with a felon.

18 QUINCY: I didn't say I was a felon. Did I say I was a felon?
19   All charges were dropped.

20 DAVEY: *(Sarcastically)* That makes me feel *so* much better.

21 TOMMY: My tooth hurts. *(Sits back down.)*

22 AHMED: Duh. That's why we're here.

23 MIGUEL: That's not why *I'm* here. My mother insists I get
24   my teeth cleaned every three months. Oral hygiene is
25   the foundation of all good health, that's what she says.

26 DAVEY: Oh, brother.

27 QUINCY: *(Stands.)* Well, I'm outta here.

28 MIGUEL: *(Increasingly suspicious)* I'm thinking the criminals
29   are outside waiting for one of us to leave.

30 QUINCY: *(Trying to bring some logic into the discussion)* Why
31   would they do that when they could come out here and
32   shoot us all in the waiting room?

33 MIGUEL: *(Seizing on this comment)* Ah ha! So you agree that
34   there are probably men with guns in the next room?

35 QUINCY: No, I'm just saying if I wanted to shoot a bunch of

1   teenagers in a waiting room —
2   TOMMY: *(Looking nauseous)* I think I'm gonna be sick.
3   DAVEY: *(Stands up.)* I tell you what, I'll go back and see if I
4   can figure out what's taking so long.
5   AHMED: You're going to just walk back there?
6   MIGUEL: Where the gun-slinging murderers are waiting?
7   TOMMY: Isn't that against the rules or something? Aren't
8   we supposed to wait out here?
9   DAVEY: We've *been* waiting. I'm going back there. *(Exits*
10   *toward backstage. Long pause. Uncomfortably long. Everyone*
11   *starts looking at each other.)*
12 MIGUEL: Just waiting for the sound of gunfire.
13 QUINCY: Wonder what's taking him so long?
14 MIGUEL: They're probably holding him hostage now.
15 AHMED: This is the dumbest thing I've ever seen.
16 QUINCY: I give him two more minutes and then I'm calling
17   the police.
18 AHMED: For what? To report that the dentist is carrying a
19   drill without a permit?
20 MIGUEL: Maybe they've used a silencer.
21 QUINCY: I think we should call the police.
22 TOMMY: I think we should leave. *(Stands and heads to exit Off-*
23   *Stage.)*
24 MIGUEL: *(Verging on hysteria)* And leave that poor guy laying
25   back there with bullet holes in his head and no
26   paramedics on the way?
27 AHMED: *(Indicating TOMMY)* I agree with this guy here. I'm
28   outta here. *(Gets up with TOMMY to leave.)*
29 MIGUEL: Wait! You're just going to leave us here with no
30   regard for our mortal safety?
31 TOMMY: *(Considers.)* Uh, yes.
32 QUINCY: I still think we should call the police.
33 AHMED: Well, good luck with that. *(AHMED and TOMMY*
34   *leave.)*
35 MIGUEL: Well, that leaves just you and me.

1 QUINCY: Should we call the police now?

2 MIGUEL: Maybe we should — *(DAVEY enters.)*

3 DAVEY: Lunch.

4 QUINCY: What?

5 DAVEY: They're eating lunch.

6 MIGUEL: The murderers are eating lunch? What a

7   coldhearted group of thugs they are!

8 DAVEY: No, the dentist and his assistants. They're on lunch

9   break.

10 QUINCY: Lunch break? No dead bodies back there?

11 DAVEY: No, I say we had more of a chance of boring each

12   other to death out here. Hey, where are the other guys?

13 QUINCY: They panicked and left. No backbone, that's their

14   problem.

15 MIGUEL: So you're telling me that this dentist scheduled

16   five patients to be seen at the exact same time then they

17   take a lunch break?

18 DAVEY: Looks that way.

19 MIGUEL: Now *I'm* leaving.

20 QUINCY: What? After all that?

21 DAVEY: Dude, he's right. What a loser this dentist is. I'm

22   outta here, too. *(MIGUEL and DAVEY leave.)*

23 QUINCY: *(Pause. Slow smile crosses his face)* I guess that

24   means that I'm next!

15. New Friends

Topic: Three friends enter a new land.

Cast:
WILL: the commander in charge, but not necessarily the wisest or bravest
SEAN and TANYA: subordinates, but a little defiant

1 *(ALL are cowering around a door, peering outside. They are*
2 *anxious and nervous.)*
3 **SEAN: Which of us is going out first?**
4 **TANYA:** *(Nervous)* **I'm not going first.**
5 **WILL: Will you stop being such chickens?**
6 **SEAN: Great. Thanks for volunteering.**
7 **WILL:** *(Emphatically)* **I didn't volunteer.**
8 **TANYA: I thought you did.**
9 **SEAN: So did I.**
10 **WILL: I'm the commander. I should stay here and** *(Looking*
11 *for an excuse)* **secure the premises.**
12 **SEAN: Exactly what premises are those?**
13 **TANYA: You wouldn't be** *afraid,* **would you, commander?**
14 **WILL:** *(Stuttering)* **Oh, no, no, of course not.**
15 **SEAN:** *(Sarcastically)* **Didn't think so.**
16 **WILL: It's just that I don't ... I shouldn't ... I wouldn't want**
17 **to abandon you.**
18 **SEAN:** *(Encouragingly)* **Abandon, abandon.**
19 **TANYA:** *(Also encouragingly)* **Sure, we'll be fine. You go right**
20 **on out there.**
21 **WILL:** *(Regaining his composure and standing up tall)* **OK. OK.**
22 **I'm not afraid. I am, after all, Commander. I have no**
23 **fear. I am fearless. This is what I'm trained for.**
24 **SEAN:** *(To TANYA)* **Is he trying to convince us or himself?**
25 **TANYA:** *(Very anxious to get him outside)* **You go right on out**

1   there, Commander. We'll, what was it you said? Secure
2   the premises.
3 SEAN: Yeah, we got your back.
4 WILL: OK. I'm ready. I mean, we've decided these beings
5   are inferior, right? What harm could they possible do to
6   us?
7 TANYA: Right. You're exactly right. No harm. Totally safe.
8   You have a good time and I'll be right behind this
9   bulletproof wall here.
10 SEAN: Nothing to fear, Commander. All evidence indicates
11   that those creatures out there are unintelligent, low-level
12   creatures totally unable to inflict any harm to our
13   superior safety suits. I'm behind the wall here, too. You
14   go.
15 WILL: *(Sarcastically)* What did I do to deserve such a brave,
16   steadfast crew? OK, I'm going. If I'm not back at
17   fourteen hundred hours, phone home. *(He exits.)*
18 TANYA: Is that considered long distance? I don't think I can
19   get reception on my cell phone from here.
20 SEAN: Good luck, Commander. Go in peace. May the force
21   be with you. *(To TANYA)* Quick! Lock the door! They're
22   gonna slaughter him!
23 TANYA: *Right! (They push the very heavy door closed.)*

16. Stuck

Topic: Strangers are stuck together in a stopped elevator.

Cast:
BRIANNA: easily panicked, near the front of the elevator
TANYA: trying desperately to keep Brianna calm, near the front of the elevator
CLAY: a friend of Will and a funny guy
WILL: friends with Clay, an average guy
CHRISTOPHER: the voice of doom, dead center in the front of the elevator
SEAN: has dry humor, is practical and logical
JAKE: nonchalant, not easily upset, and a little clueless
CORRIN: adventure lover
GABE: average guy, very practical
BRAD: not easily upset, just a normal guy

1   *(There is no setting, but all should be obviously tightly*
2   *gathered as if on an elevator.)*
3 **BRIANNA:** *(Looking up and around. Gauging the atmosphere of*
4   *the elevator)* **Tanya, I think there's something wrong with**
5   **this elevator.**
6 **TANYA: You always think that.**
7 **CLAY: Dude, I don't think this elevator is moving.**
8 **WILL: Of course it is. You get on an elevator and it takes**
9   **you up or down. That's the plan.**
10 **CHRISTOPHER:** *(Very dark, very low, very ominous)*
11   **Something is terribly, terribly wrong.**
12 **SEAN: Excuse me, does anyone else feel like this elevator**
13   **is not moving?**
14 **JAKE: Sure it is. It's fine. Don't say that.**
15 **BRAD: I'm really gonna be late now.**
16 **CHRISTOPHER:** *(Saying what everyone's thinking)* **It's not**
17   **moving. We're stuck. We're stuck here forever.**
18 **TANYA: Don't say that. It will be fine. It's probably only**

1   stuck for a minute.

2 GABE: You don't know that.

3 CORRIN: This is cool.

4 BRIANNA: *(Getting upset and spooked)* It's not cool. I hate
5   these things. This is very upsetting to me.

6 TANYA; *(Trying to calm her down)* Calm down, Brianna, just
7   calm down.

8 CHRISTOPHER: I knew something like this was going to
9   happen today. We're all going to die in here.

10 SEAN: *(Voice of reason)* Hey, isn't there a phone or
11   something we can use to call for help?

12 BRAD: I don't have a cell phone. Do you have a cell phone?
13   I knew I should have gotten a cell phone. It's for times
14   just like this that everyone really should have a cell
15   phone.

16 SEAN: I was talking about the elevator phone.

17 CLAY: What's an elevator phone?

18 GABE: Oh, yeah, that phone that you're supposed to use in
19   case of an emergency.

20 CORRIN: This isn't an emergency. We're just stuck a little.
21   It'll be fine.

22 WILL: How can you be stuck *a little* in an elevator?

23 CHRISTOPHER: *(Continuing in his gloomy predictions)* If we
24   don't suffocate, then the cables will probably snap and
25   the whole car will plummet to the ground and we'll all be
26   crushed.

27 GABE: Have you thought about looking into a little therapy?

28 BRIANNA: *(The atmosphere is beginning to get edgy.)* I think
29   I'm going to faint.

30 TANYA: You're not going to faint. Calm down. Everybody
31   just calm down.

32 JAKE: Does anybody have anything to eat?

33 CLAY: What?

34 JAKE: I didn't eat breakfast.

35 SEAN: *Soooo* how's it coming with that elevator telephone?

1   TANYA: There isn't one.

2   SEAN: There isn't one?

3   TANYA: No, there's no phone.

4   SEAN: I thought there was supposed to be a phone.

5   TANYA: Maybe there is *supposed* to be a phone, but there

6   isn't one here.

7   WILL: Great.

8   CHRISTOPHER: *(In anguish)* And the last thing I said to my

9   mother was, "You're not nice to me." What kind of last

10   words are they? The rest of her life she'll be haunted by

11   her dead son saying, "You're not nice to me." I could

12   have said "I love you." That would have been the best

13   last words. Those are the best last words anyone can

14   say, "I love you."

15 CLAY: *(Trying to be silly)* Hey, Will, I love you.

16 WILL: *(Not appreciating the attempt)* Cut it out. You're

17   disgusting.

18 BRAD: Would somebody do something?

19 SEAN: *(Trying to be logical and practical)* Does anyone have

20   any skills that would help us get out of here?

21 JAKE: I can cook an omelet.

22 GABE: Very helpful. Come on, guys, think.

23 CHRISTOPHER: *(Monotonously, hands raised, saying last rites*

24   *for all in the elevator)* Though I walk through the valley of

25   the shadow of death, I shall fear no evil ...

26 CLAY: Oh, I saw a movie where they climbed out through the

27   ceiling. *(ALL look up and pause.)*

28 GABE: Any other ideas?

29 JAKE: Well, we could call for help on my cell phone.

30 TANYA: You've got a cell phone?!

31 JAKE: *(Holds it up.)* Sure, right here.

32 SEAN: Somebody take that phone away from that kid so I

33   can strangle him.

34 GABE: Give me that phone you goofball.

35 BRIANNA: Wait! Did you feel that?

1 CHRISTOPHER: This is it. God bless each of you.

2 WILL: I think we're moving.

3 BRIANNA: Up or down? *(A little panicked)* Up or down?!

4 BRAD: Calm down, girl. Up. We're going up.

5 TANYA: See? I told you it would be OK.

6 CORRIN: Oh, shoot. It's moving all right.

7 SEAN: I'm going to need a lot of therapy after this.

8 CHRISTOPHER: *(Shocked)* You mean we're not going to die?

9 CLAY: *(Just about had it with CHRISTOPHER)* If you don't shut
10   up, I won't be able to guarantee that.

11 CHRISTOPHER: You mean the elevator is not going to
12   crash?

13 WILL: It certainly looks that way. Look! The door's opening!

14 BRAD: Oh, I guess I'm not going to be late after all.

15 CORRIN: We were only in here like three minutes.

16 GABE: *(Points to CHRISTOPHER)* With this guy, it seemed
17   *much* longer.

18 BRIANNA: It's going to be all right. It's all going to be fine.
19   Everybody, we're OK!

20 CHRISTOPHER: I gotta call my mother. *(Runs out.)*

21 JAKE: I hope that snack shop is still open *(Exits.)*

22 TANYA: Come on, Brianna, you need a nice, warm cup of
23   hot chocolate. *(BRIANNA and TANYA exit.)*

24 CORRIN: Shoot, I was hoping we'd be on the news and all.
25   *(CORRIN, CLAY, and WILL exit.)*

26 BRAD: Nice, uh, being stuck with you. *(Exits.)*

27 GABE: What a group. *(Exits.)*

28 SEAN: It's days like today that make it a waste of energy to
29   get out of bed.

17. Lady-Killers

Topic: The awkwardness of a middle school mixer from the perspective of the guys.

Cast:
WILL: fun-loving, afraid of the girls
CORY: cute and full of his own cuteness
JAKE: typically more interested than brave

1   *(The BOYS are sitting in folding chairs that are in a straight*
2   *line, gazing across the stage.)*
3   **WILL:** *(Dejectedly)* **There is absolutely no way.**
4   **CORY:** *(Similarly sad)* **You're right. No way.**
5   **JAKE:** *(Also sad)* **It's just not gonna happen.** *(Pause. BOYS*
6   *resituate, check cell phones, roll sleeves up, fidget, look*
7   *around, etc., to indicate they are really bored.)*
8   **WILL: So, what are we gonna do?**
9   **JAKE: I have no idea.** *(Pause. They fidget again.)*
10 **CORY: We could just sit here for the next three hours.**
11 **WILL: That sounds like lots of fun.** *(Pause. They fidget.)*
12 **JAKE: Maybe one of us should give it a try.**
13 **WILL: Yeah, right. You volunteering, Jake?**
14 **JAKE: Not me. I thought maybe Cory would want to —**
15 **CORY: Yeah, forget it.**
16 **JAKE: Yeah, you're right.**
17 **WILL: We'll just have to sit here, then.**
18 **CORY: OK, I guess that's our only option at this point.**
19   *(Pause. They fidget.)*
20 **JAKE: This is stupid.**
21 **WILL: You can say that again.**
22 **JAKE: This is stupid.**
23 **CORY: Don't encourage him.**
24 **JAKE: I'm bored.**

1 WILL: We're all bored. Just shut up and sit there. *(Pause.*
2 *They fidget.)*
3 CORY: That one with the green jacket is cute.
4 WILL: Good luck, Cory.
5 CORY: I'm not going anywhere.
6 JAKE: *(Teasingly)* She's looking at you.
7 CORY: She is not.
8 WILL: *(Agreeing)* Yeah, I think she's looking at you, Cory.
9 CORY: No way.
10 JAKE: She wants you to come over and ask her to dance.
11 CORY: What are you now, like, an expert on girls?
12 JAKE: *(Getting into it)* You can just tell. She keeps looking
13   at you.
14 CORY: *(Very pleased with the idea)* Well, I am super good-
15   looking.
16 WILL: *(Not as impressed)* Oh please. She probably thinks you
17   have something growing out of your head or something.
18 CORY: She's not looking at you, though, is she?
19 JAKE: No, she's looking at Cory. Hey! Here she comes!
20 CORY: Tell me she's not coming over here.
21 WILL: She's coming over here.
22 CORY: I asked you not to tell me that!
23 JAKE: What are you gonna do?
24 CORY: I don't know.
25 WILL: You know, you could bite the bullet and dance with
26   her.
27 CORY: No way!
28 JAKE: *(Sarcastically)* Yeah, Will, how stupid can you get? I
29   mean we came to this dance specifically so we could sit
30   in the corner with a couple of other guys and *not* dance
31   with girls.
32 CORY: *(Starting to panic)* She's still coming! What am I
33   gonna do?
34 WILL: She could be really nice. And she's cute. You should
35   dance with her.

1   CORY: I don't know how to dance!

2   WILL: Maybe you should have thought of that before you

3   came tonight!

4   JAKE: Hey, guys, the path is clear. Twenty feet and we're

5   out of here!

6   CORY: I'm right behind you! Let's go! *(They run out.)*

18. The Eighteenth Year

Topic: A cicada bug misses her entrance by a year.

Cast:
BRIANNA: a seventeenth year cicada bug; cheerful, naïve, anxious to make new friends
CLIFF and JAMAL: slightly sarcastic and sardonic bugs trying to be friendly

1 **BRIANNA:** *(Very cheerful, full of energy)* **Well, hi there, guys.**
2 **CLIFF:** *(To JAMAL in a stage whisper)* **What in the heck is**
3   **that?**
4 **JAMAL:** *(To CLIFF)* **It looks like one of those seventeenth**
5   **year cicadas who were here last year.**
6 **BRIANNA: Am I late?**
7 **CLIFF: If you are what we think you are, then yeah, you're**
8   **a little late.**
9 **JAMAL: Like a whole year.**
10 **BRIANNA:** *(Shocked)* **A year? What? That can't be!**
11 **CLIFF: Women. Never on time.**
12 **JAMAL: What happened?**
13 **BRIANNA: Well ... I don't know ... I thought I was supposed**
14   **to come up now.**
15 **JAMAL: Last year.**
16 **CLIFF: You're only off by a year. Don't feel bad.**
17 **BRIANNA: Oh, goodness, how could this have happened?**
18   *(Thinking it over. Obviously very upset)* **Oh, dear! What am**
19   **I going to do? Everyone's gone and I'm a whole year late!**
20 **CLIFF:** *(Trying to console her)* **Oh, don't be upset. It's not that**
21   **bad.**
22 **BRIANNA:** *(Through her tears)* **It's not?**
23 **JAMAL: No, you didn't miss much last year.**
24 **CLIFF: Yeah, everyone was so grossed out by the thousands**

1   and thousands of your friends, they never would have
2   appreciated your ... *(Looking for a nice word)* **uniqueness.**
3 **BRIANNA:** *(Sounding hopeful)* **My uniqueness?**
4 **JAMAL: Sure. You have a beautiful** ... *(Searching for*
5   *something nice)* **um ... purple body.**
6 **CLIFF: And such lovely ... unique ... effervescent wings.**
7 **BRIANNA:** *(Preening)* **Do you think so?**
8 **CLIFF:** *(On a roll)* **Sure! You'll be the talk of the town. And**
9   **just think of all the people who missed the whole thing**
10   **last year. Maybe they were away or something and didn't**
11   **get to see your friends. You'll be special.**
12 **BRIANNA:** *(Shyly proud)* **I always thought I was a little**
13   **special.**
14 **JAMAL: Sure you are! Why don't you fly on over to that park**
15   **and find some people to annoy — I mean, show off for.**
16 **BRIANNA: OK, I will! Thanks, guys!** *(She exits.)*
17 **JAMAL: Wait 'til they get a load of her!**
18 **CLIFF: And those stupid people thought they were through**
19   **with those disgusting things for another seventeen**
20   **years!**

19. Mad Cow Disease

Topic: Two cows discuss human behavior from their perspective.

Cast:
CLOVER
BUTTERCUP

Costumes
Students do not need to dress as cows but may. A simple costume would be white sweats with black patches and headband with ears. They stand, not crawl on all fours.

1   *(CLOVER and BUTTERCUP are Center Stage.)*
2   **CLOVER:** 'Sup?
3   **BUTTERCUP:** Not much.
4   **CLOVER:** You see that new donkey they got next door?
5   **BUTTERCUP:** Yeah, a real winner. Donkeys have got to be
6   the dumbest animals ever created on God's green earth.
7   **CLOVER:** You got that right. I saw him out in the field
8   chewing on a tennis ball, just as happy as can be. Those
9   stupid animals will eat anything.
10 **BUTTERCUP:** I heard Old Ginger was gonna be shown at the
11   state fair next month.
12 **CLOVER:** *(Laughs.)* Oh, yeah, you should have seen what
13   they did to her. Gave her a sweet little haircut and
14   braided her tail.
15 **BUTTERCUP:** *(Laughs.)* How humiliating. I'm glad I was
16   never chosen to go the fair.
17 **CLOVER:** It's bad enough that we get those school tours.
18 **BUTTERCUP:** Oh, you should have seen that group that
19   came through last week. They came into the milking
20   station and this little kid yells, "Hey, is that a girl cow
21   or a boy cow?"
22 **CLOVER:** That's nothing. How about the people riding by in

1   their cars? It never fails. They roll down their windows
2   and yell, "Moooo!" They think they're so clever.
3 BUTTERCUP: Well, they are only humans. You've gotta feel
4   sorry for them.
5 CLOVER: You're right. They put those stupid clothes all over
6   their body — sometimes they can hardly walk. And they
7   have such wimpy feet that they have to cover them all
8   the time. You ever seen one get mud on one of those foot
9   covers?
10 BUTTERCUP: Oh, yeah, they go all nuts, scraping them on
11   the fence, cursing all the time. What do they think is
12   gonna get on their feet when they walk into a field? Hello!
13 CLOVER: No, my favorite part is when it rains.
14 BUTTERCUP: Yeah, please explain this to me. They spend
15   all their money installing the most expensive showers
16   and pools and going to the beach to swim. They stick
17   their clothes into the washing machine every day. But
18   heaven forbid it should rain on them.
19 CLOVER: They turn tail and run back to their cars like they
20   were on fire!
21 BUTTERCUP: You do have to feel sorry for them. Have you
22   ever seen that slop they eat?
23 CLOVER: Ew, all they eat is stuff that comes wrapped in
24   paper with gold arches on it. It smells disgusting.
25 BUTTERCUP: Give me a good old bag of oats any time.
26 CLOVER: And give me a nice thunderstorm any day. Cool,
27   refreshing rain. Gets all the dirt off, cools us down.
28   Those humans are just plain stupid.
29 BUTTERCUP: Well, at least we've got them trained.
30 CLOVER: Yep. Everyday, crack of dawn, they're out here
31   cleaning up our stalls and bringing us fresh food. We've
32   got the good life, I'm telling you.
33 BUTTERCUP: Have you heard of that thing called "mad cow
34   disease?"
35 CLOVER: I wouldn't exactly call it a disease. I get mad all

1   the time.

2   BUTTERCUP: Yeah, me, too. I don't know what they're

3   talking about.

4   CLOVER: Hey, if it turns one more human into a vegetarian,

5   I'm all for promoting it.

6   BUTTERCUP: Good point! Let's spread the word. Tell all our

7   friends to act like they have this "mad cow disease" and

8   the humans will totally leave us alone!

9   CLOVER: Let's go!

20. Clowning Around

Topic: Two friends discuss a common problem.

Cast:
JULES: reasonable, likes to tease
EVIE: terrified by clowns

1   *(JULES and EVIE sit on a sofa or chairs.)*
2   JULES: Who's afraid of clowns?
3   EVIE: Everyone is.
4   JULES: No, no one is afraid of clowns. They paint clowns on
5   nursery walls.
6   EVIE: *(Getting upset just thinking about it)* **Yeah, and then, at**
7   **night, the demon clowns come alive and scare the little**
8   **babies. That's why no one likes clowns.**
9   JULES: You're crazy. All kids like clowns. You're just weird.
10 EVIE: I'm telling you, if you took a poll, ninety percent of
11   people are afraid of clowns.
12 JULES: Then why are they still at every single circus?
13 EVIE: You go to the circus?
14 JULES: No. Not since I was five.
15 EVIE: Why?
16 JULES: I don't know. My parents don't like the circus.
17 EVIE: They probably don't like the clowns.
18 JULES: They don't like the elephant poop.
19 EVIE: I mean it. You should ask them. I bet they're afraid of
20   the clowns.
21 JULES: Look, Evie. Clowns are funny. They fall and throw
22   pies at each other. They make people laugh. They paint
23   big smiles on their faces. They're always happy. What in
24   the world is there to be afraid of clowns for?
25 EVIE: I can't describe it. They have those evil permanent ink
26   smiles, like they're smiling but they're planning on

1   murdering you in your sleep.

2 JULES: Where do you get these things?

3 EVIE: Didn't you ever see that movie? What was the name?

4 JULES: Raggedy Ann?

5 EVIE: No, that horror movie with the clown.

6 JULES: No one made a horror film about a clown. That's
7   ridiculous.

8 EVIE: No, no, I'm telling you. It was really creepy. *It*.

9 JULES: What's it?

10 EVIE: The movie. It's called *It*.

11 JULES: There's no movie called *It*.

12 EVIE: There is too. It's about this evil clown that comes
13   alive and kills everyone.

14 JULES: Well, at least I know what I'm going to get you for
15   your birthday.

16 EVIE: Don't you dare. I'll never speak to you again.

17 JULES: *(Sighs.)* I'm tired of this. Let's go to the mall.

18 EVIE: OK. *(Pause) Wait.* Which mall?

19 JULES: I don't care. Why?

20 EVIE: Towson. We have to go to Towson.

21 JULES: Fine. But maybe we should go to White Marsh.
22   There's a —

23 EVIE: *Clown!* There's a clown at White Marsh Mall.

24 JULES: *(Exasperated)* Oh, good grief.

25 EVIE: She walks around with this huge bunch of balloons.
26   She looks nice, but she's not.

27 JULES: I think you're seriously disturbed. But fine, Towson
28   is fine.

29 EVIE: OK, I'll get my jacket. *(Exits.)*

30 JULES: *(To self)* I guess we should go in the back entrance.
31   The shoeshine kid at the front might freak her out. But
32   wait, they have that coin-operated pony at the back
33   entrance. She probably couldn't handle that, either.

34 EVIE: *(Enters.)* OK, let's go.

35 JULES: You're sure you're up to this? There might be toy

1   soldiers or rabid hamsters at Towson Mall.

2   EVIE: Oh, ha ha. It's only clowns. There are no clowns at
3   Towson Mall.

4   JULES: What about elves? I think there are elves with
5   Santa.

6   EVIE: *(Not amused)* Just clowns.

7   JULES: OK, just checking. You never know what evil might
8   lurk within the heart of an elf or a Panda Express sales
9   clerk.

10 EVIE: I never thought of that. Let's just stay here and play
11   video games.

12 JULES: *(Sighs.)* Fine. I'll call for pizza.

13 EVIE: *No!* Didn't you see that movie where the pizza guy —

14 JULES: *Go home!*

21. Misunderstanding

Topic: Friends work through a problem of communication.

Cast:
JOANIE: wants to be the peacekeeper
GABE: bitter, angry at Monica and Marcel
MONICA: nice, unsure of the problem
MARCEL: unaware of Gabe's anger

1   *(The scene opens with JOANIE and GABE Stage Left, talking*
2   *so that the kids on the other side of the stage cannot hear*
3   *them. MONICA and MARCEL are sitting with heads together*
4   *working on a list, quietly talking.)*
5   **JOANIE:** *(Trying to be convincing)* **Let's just go over and ask**
6   **if we can hang with them.**
7   **GABE:** *(Adamant)* **No way. Forget it.**
8   **JOANIE: Come on, Gabe, I'm tired of all this.**
9   **GABE: Well, you can go. I'm staying right here.**
10 **JOANIE: You're impossible, you know that? You're so**
11   **stubborn!**
12 **GABE: Leave me alone. Go hang with them. I couldn't care**
13   **less.**
14 **JOANIE: Fine.** *(She walks to MONICA and MARCEL. GABE sits*
15   *and pouts.)*
16 **MONICA:** *(Upbeat and friendly)* **Hi, Joanie! How's it going?**
17 **JOANIE:** *(Hesitantly)* **Fine. I guess.**
18 **MARCEL: You don't sound fine. Something wrong?**
19 **JOANIE: No. I guess not. What are you doing?** *(Keeps*
20   *glancing at GABE, who is sulking.)*
21 **MONICA: We're making up the list for the Christmas**
22   **exchange. How much do you think we should each**
23   **spend?**
24 **JOANIE:** *(Dull, without interest, and unaware)* **I don't know.**

1 MARCEL: I say a million dollars each. What do you say,
2   Joanie?
3 JOANIE: *(Obviously more interested in GABE and not following*
4   *the conversation)* Hmmmm? Sure, that's fine.
5 MONICA: *(Waves hand in front of JOANIE's face.)* Earth to
6   Joanie. Anybody home in there?
7 JOANIE: *(Comes back to awareness.)* Oh, sorry guys, I'm a
8   little distracted.
9 MARCEL: Obviously. What's wrong, and don't say nothing?
10 JOANIE: Nothing.
11 MARCEL: I told you not to say that!
12 MONICA: What's wrong with Gabe?
13 MARCEL: Yeah, he's been avoiding me all day.
14 JOANIE: *(Hesitantly)* Yeah, well ...
15 MONICA: *(Impatiently)* Well ... what?
16 JOANIE: You know.
17 MONICA: Know what?
18 JOANIE: About the party.
19 MARCEL: *(Confused)* Party?
20 JOANIE: Yeah. We're both pretty upset about the party.
21 MARCEL: *(Completely confused)* OK, I feel like we're having a
22   conversation in code. What are you talking about?
23 JOANIE: The party. Monica's party. Gabe is mad he wasn't
24   invited. I am too, a little.
25 MONICA: What do you mean you weren't invited?
26 JOANIE: Not invited, like didn't receive an invitation, like
27   everyone else in the whole class got one except Gabe
28   and me.
29 MARCEL: I *knew* he was mad at me!
30 MONICA: *(Desperate to clear this up)* Oh, Joanie, you're
31   invited! When you didn't RSVP I thought it was because
32   you didn't want to come.
33 JOANIE: *(Confused and defensive)* I didn't get an invitation.
34 MARCEL: Did you look in your locker?
35 JOANIE: Sure, but my locker was moved because of the
36   water leak.

1 MONICA: You don't have locker two-fourteen?
2 JOANIE: No, locker three-thirty-one.
3 MONICA: Well, that explains why you didn't get the
4   invitation.
5 MARCEL: It's probably still floating in locker two-fourteen.
6   Let's go talk to Gabe. *(They all cross to GABE, hesitantly.)*
7 MONICA: Gabe, there's been a —
8 GABE: *(He's been saving it up and now he lets loose.)* I can't
9   believe you're talking to me. You embarrassed me in
10   front of everyone. Jimmy asks me, "You going to
11   Monica's party?" and I say, "What party?" and he says,
12   "Oh, I guess you weren't invited." I gotta tell you, I felt
13   like an idiot. And you can just have your stupid party. I
14   wouldn't go anyway. I'd just as soon stay at home and
15   play with my little sister — at least I know she won't
16   stab me in the back. I can't believe you —
17 MARCEL: *(Interrupting. Shouts.)* *Timeout! Breathe!* You're
18   gonna give yourself an aneurysm, Gabe!
19 MONICA: You have locker two-fifteen, right?
20 GABE: No.
21 MARCEL: Don't tell me — water damage?
22 GABE: *(Suspiciously)* Yeah, what do you care?
23 MARCEL: I'll guess your invitation is floating in there along
24   with Joanie's.
25 GABE: What?
26 JOANIE: They say they stuck it through the slats on our old
27   lockers. They didn't know we switched.
28 GABE: *(Obviously does not believe it)* Yeah, sure. And you
29   believed them?
30 JOANIE: Why not?
31 MARCEL: *(Starting to get a little upset herself)* You can prove it
32   if you think you have to. Go take a dip in your old
33   lockers and look for the invitations.
34 MONICA: *(Not happy about the way things are going)* I can't
35   believe you thought we didn't invite you. And you didn't

1   say anything, you just assumed the worst.
2   GABE: *(Beginning to realize his mistake)* **Yeah, well ...**
3   MONICA: Now *I'm* upset.
4   JOANIE: I'm sorry, Monica, I shouldn't have just assumed.
5   MARCEL: Yeah, Gabe, why didn't you just ask?
6   GABE: Sure, like, "Hey, Marcel, why wasn't I invited?"
7   Right.
8   MARCEL: Exactly. I would have asked you if it were the
9   other way around.
10   JOANIE: I guess we didn't have all the facts.
11   GABE: Yeah, I guess I should have asked.
12   MONICA: Yeah, you should have. Well?
13   GABE: Well what?
14   MONICA: Are you coming?
15   GABE: Sure, I wouldn't miss it for the world!
16   MARCEL: Sure your little sister won't mind?
17   GABE: You kidding? I can't stand that little pest!
18   MONICA: I nominate Gabe and Joanie for the clean-up
19   committee! *(They start walking off.)*
20   MARCEL: I second that nomination!
21   JOANIE: Hey, wait a minute!

22. Gossip among Friends

Topic: A play based on the harm that can come from gossip.

Cast:
SUSAN: anxious to share gossip
MARY: not as gossipy as Susan
JEFF: the voice of reason

1 *(Scene opens with SUSAN and MARY standing Center Stage*
2 *deep in conversation.)*
3 SUSAN: Well, that's what she said.
4 MARY: Are you sure she wasn't talking about Jimmy?
5 SUSAN: No. I heard her say Adam three times in the
6 conversation. I know she wasn't talking about Jimmy.
7 MARY: Well, somebody really should tell Jimmy.
8 JEFF: *(Enters and joins SUSAN and MARY, overhearing the end*
9 *of the last line.)* Tell Jimmy what?
10 SUSAN: *(Pretending innocence)* Oh, nothing.
11 JEFF: Come on, I heard you say somebody should tell
12 Jimmy and he's one of our best friends. What is it he
13 should know?
14 SUSAN: *(Suddenly hesitant to talk)* I don't think it's my place
15 to say.
16 MARY: Oh, that's a switch. Now you don't want to be
17 caught gossiping.
18 SUSAN: It was different when I was telling you. But if I tell
19 Jeff ...
20 JEFF: *(Offended)* If you tell Jeff what? Are you saying I'm a
21 blabbermouth?
22 SUSAN: No, it's just that you and Jimmy are good friends
23 and I don't want this getting back to him.
24 MARY: Well, maybe it should get back to him. It would be for
25 his own good if he knew. You know how sensitive Jimmy is.

1 SUSAN: That's just the reason why he should know what
2   people are saying about him.
3 JEFF: *(Frustrated)* What are they saying about him?
4 SUSAN: OK, Jeff, if someone heard someone say that they
5   had heard someone say you were seen by someone else
6   smoking cigarettes, would you want that someone to tell
7   you they had heard it?
8 JEFF: *(Completely confused)* If ... if who someone heard a
9   someone do *what?*
10 SUSAN: See, I told you it was stupid.
11 MARY: It's not stupid. You're just not explaining it right.
12   Jeff, if one of your friends heard something bad about
13   you, wouldn't you want to know?
14 JEFF: Well, that depends.
15 MARY: On what?!
16 JEFF: *(Being deliberately confusing)* On whether they actually
17   saw or heard something or whether their cousin's
18   brother's friend's dentist's secretary's dog heard it.
19 MARY: *(Absolutely lost)* What?
20 SUSAN: I think he's trying to say that gossip never helped
21   anyone, right?
22 JEFF: Right!

23. The Snob

Topic: A play about judging a book by its cover.

Cast:
JOSEPH: cheerful and friendly
DIMITRI: obviously bitter and angry
CATHY: polite but confused by Dimitri

1   *(Scene begins with DIMITRI sitting alone, brooding. JOSEPH*
2   *enters and joins him.)*
3   JOSEPH: Hey, Dimitri, what's up?
4   DIMITRI: *(Gloomily)* I don't want to talk about it.
5   JOSEPH: Come on, it's me. You can talk to me. What's
6   wrong?
7   DIMITRI: That new girl in guitar class is *so* stuck up.
8   JOSEPH: *(Sits beside him. Seems curious)* Who, Cathy? I
9   thought she was pretty cool.
10 DIMITRI: Yeah, well, you didn't go to grade school with her.
11   Her father is like president of the world and her mom
12   drives a Lamborghini. She's so rich it's ridiculous.
13 JOSEPH: So what? What's rich got to do with anything?
14   She's always really nice.
15 DIMITRI: Shhhh! Here she comes. *(CATHY enters and joins the*
16   *BOYS, but does not sit.)*
17 CATHY: Hi, Joseph. Hi, Dimitri.
18 JOSEPH: Hey, Cathy.
19 DIMITRI: *(Grouchy, not looking at her)* Hmph.
20 CATHY: *(Genuinely concerned)* Is something wrong, Dimitri?
21 DIMITRI: No, nothing's wrong. Everything is just peachy
22   keen.
23 JOSEPH: Ignore him, Cathy. He hasn't had his breakfast
24   today.
25 CATHY: I tried to get your attention during guitar class,
26   Dimitri. When Mr. Reynolds said, "OK, musicians!"

1   didn't that remind you of old Mr. Talbot in grade school?

2 DIMITRI: Hmph.

3 CATHY: *(Hesitantly, still trying to make conversation)* I mean,

4   like he used to call us "musicians" all the time,

5   remember that?

6 DIMITRI: Whatever. *(Dreadful silence. DIMITRI broods, JOSEPH*

7   *shakes his head disgustedly, CATHY lingers confused.)*

8 CATHY: Well, I guess I'd better go wait for my mom over

9   there. See you guys. *(She walks away slowly, glancing*

10   *back at the boys.)*

11 JOSEPH: *(He calls after her.)* Bye, Cathy! *(Then to DIMITRI)*

12   Man, could you have been more rude?

13 DIMITRI: *(Faking surprise. Defensive)* What? I didn't do

14   anything!

15 JOSEPH: She was trying to be all nice and make polite

16   conversation and you couldn't say one word to her.

17 DIMITRI: I did too say one word. I said "whatever."

18 JOSEPH: Yeah, right. Whatever. Hey, Cathy, wait up! *(He*

19   *exits, leaving DIMITRI alone looking a little ashamed.)*

24. A Kennel of Truth

Topic: Three dogs discuss differing perspectives of the local kennel visit.

Cast:
MACK: super hyper, way too happy, kind of like a Jack Russell Terrier
REGGIE: cynical, been around the doghouse a couple of times, kind of like a Sheepdog
BULL'S EYE: older, lazy, not real impressed with the new kid, kind of like a Bassett Hound

Costumes
Optional, but can be easily designed using sweats, T-shirts, and ears on headbands. Face paint is also fun. Should be performed on two legs, not on all fours.

1   *(Scene opens with REGGIE and BULL'S EYE lying around*
2   *lazily, obviously bored and not happy. MACK should come in*
3   *with very high energy.)*
4   **MACK:** *(Extremely happy)* **Hey, guys, what's up?**
5   **REGGIE:** *(Opposite tone of MACK)* **You're a little too chipper.**
6   **BULL'S EYE:** *(Not happy to have his nap disturbed)* **Yeah, what**
7   **do you have to be so happy about?**
8   **MACK:** *(Super psyched)* **Vacation! Party on! We're on**
9   **vacation!**
10 **REGGIE: That's what they're calling it these days?**
11 **MACK: Sure, vacation! Fun times, good friends, party**
12   **games!**
13 **BULL'S EYE:** *(Sarcastically)* **What planet are you from?**
14 **MACK: Oh, your masters must not have told you about all**
15   **the fun we're gonna have. Is this your first time on**
16   **vacation?**
17 **BULL'S EYE: No, Mack, it's my eleventh.**
18 **REGGIE: My sixth. Your first and, let me guess** *(Letting*
19   *MACK in on the harsh realities of life),* **your master told you**

1   *vacation* was all good times, huh?

2 MACK: *(Still very excited. Obviously well-prepared for this*

3   *vacation)* Sure! Frisbee, swimming in the lake, playing

4   with friends, fetch, lots of food, sleep all day if I want.

5   That's what I call vacation!

6 REGGIE: *(Shaking head)* Yeah, that's what you call Fantasy

7   Land.

8 BULL'S EYE: Reality check, bud.

9 MACK: Huh?

10 REGGIE: This is a kennel, you dope.

11 MACK: Right. "Krazy Kanine Kamp," vacation boarding. I'm

12   excited.

13 BULL'S EYE: The name might be, let's say, a little

14   misleading.

15 REGGIE: Yeah, more like "Dismal Days Doing Diddly-squat."

16 REGGIE: Yeah. Not much partying going on here, pal. Sorry.

17 MACK: *(Slightly disillusioned)* No Frisbee?

18 REGGIE: I think there's an old boot in the back alley.

19 MACK: *(Even more disturbed)* No swimming?

20 BULL'S EYE: They spray you down before you go home so

21   you don't stink.

22 MACK: *(Increasingly concerned)* No good food?

23 BULL'S EYE: No *good* food. A little *lousy* food.

24 MACK: *(Horror of horrors)* Sleep?

25 REGGIE: *(Conceding this point)* Yeah, you get to sleep.

26 BULL'S EYE: Sleep all you want.

27 MACK: *(Looking at the bright side)* Well, that's not too bad.

28 BULL'S EYE: Yeah, you're right about that.

29 MACK: *(Pointing out the glass is half full)* Lots of snoozing and

30   good pals to talk to. I'll take that over lying around the

31   house waiting for Dad to come home all day with nothing

32   to do but chase the stupid cat.

33 REGGIE: *(Suddenly awake and fascinated)* You have a *cat?*

34 MACK: *(Disgustedly)* Yeah. What an idiot. Who would ever

35   bring a cat home when they had one of us?

1 BULL'S EYE: *(Also finally interested in the conversation)* **Good**
2   **question. Tell us about your stupid cat. This will be fun!**
3 MACK: See! I told you we would have a fun vacation!
4 REGGIE: Yeah, maybe you're right. Is it a calico cat?
5 MACK: No, a stupid red tabby with a missing tail! *(They all*
6   *laugh.)*

25. The Class Party

Topic: Students try to plan a class party.

Cast:
NADIA: motherly, bossy
BEN: lazy, uncooperative
EBONEE: full of energy, fun-loving
ZECHARIAH: practical, does not enjoy the process
MILAN: the brain trust of the group
TAYLOR: the second boss with high energy and lots of ideas
BLAIR: bored but can be talked into cooperating

1 *(Scene begins with ALL sitting together in a group. NADIA*
2 *has a pad and pencil. Others can have school props to play*
3 *with: pencils, books, calculators, etc.)*
4 **NADIA:** *(Already a little exasperated)* **OK, we're supposed to**
5 **be working on this list. Anybody have any suggestions?**
6 **BEN:** *(Bored)* **I don't feel like doing this.**
7 **EBONEE:** *(Obviously a social butterfly)* **Come on, it will be fun.**
8 **We could have a great party if we just put a little**
9 **thought into it.**
10 **ZECHARIAH:** *(Obviously wishing the session was over)* **I wish**
11 **she would just tell us what to bring.**
12 **TAYLOR:** *(Adding his input)* **No, this is more fun. We get to**
13 **decide for ourselves what we're gonna do at the party.**
14 **Isn't that more fun?**
15 **MILAN:** *(Almost mechanical, like a computer)* **The process of**
16 **determining our own supplies and entertainment for our**
17 **festivities would be a very beneficial and rewarding**
18 **activity.**
19 **BLAIR:** *(Confused by MILAN's big words)* **What did he say?**
20 **BEN: Is it lunch time yet?**
21 **NADIA:** *(Trying to bring them back on topic)* **Come on, guys,**
22 **we have to get working on this.**

1 TAYLOR: I can bring all my CDs. I have a ton of CDs and my
2   music is really cool.
3 ZECHARIAH: *(Dryly)* Depends on what you mean by *cool.*
4 BEN: Got any heavy metal?
5 BLAIR: *(Disgusted)* Ew. Not heavy metal.
6 EBONEE: Forget about the music. What are we gonna eat?
7 BEN: Yeah, what are we gonna eat?
8 ZECHARIAH: Can't we just order pizza?
9 TAYLOR: We get pizza every Friday. Can't we think of
10   something different?
11 MILAN: We might take this opportunity to explore different
12   dietary options.
13 EBONEE: *(Confused)* When you start talking like that I don't
14   understand a bit of what you're saying.
15 BLAIR: He said we should try something different.
16 BEN: He did?
17 TAYLOR: I don't like different. I like pizza.
18 NADIA: And I like salsa music, but I don't think you'd go for
19   that, would you?
20 ZECHARIAH: What in the world is *salsa?*
21 TAYLOR: My music collection is great. We should listen to
22   my CDs.
23 BEN: *(Suddenly inspired)* Fried chicken.
24 NADIA: What?
25 BEN: We should eat fried chicken.
26 BLAIR: *(Disgusted)* That's full of bad trans fats. I don't eat
27   that garbage.
28 BEN: I *live* on that garbage. It's good!
29 NADIA: We could get salad with the pizzas.
30 TAYLOR: *(Appalled)* Salad? What kind of party is this,
31   anyway?
32 EBONEE: Any party that has salad can no longer be called
33   a party.
34 MILAN: If we supplement the more unhealthy food choices
35   with vegetables or other healthy alternatives, it could

1   counteract the negative effects of the less healthy
2   selections.
3 EBONEE: Is he speaking English?
4 NADIA: Come on, guys, we're never gonna get this done.
5 TAYLOR: And then the teacher will plan the whole thing for
6   us.
7 ZECHARIAH: *(Inspired)* That was my plan from the start! We
8   could have saved all this trouble!
9 BLAIR: Trouble? You think planning a party is trouble?
10 BEN: With you guys it is.
11 EBONEE: All this talking about food is making me hungry.
12 BEN: Is it lunchtime?
13 MILAN: There are still twelve minutes and forty-one seconds
14   left before lunch.
15 TAYLOR: We didn't even talk about decorations yet.
16 BEN: This is really sounding like a girly party.
17 BLAIR: Why? Because we want decorations?
18 NADIA: I give up.
19 ZECHARIAH: You all wake me up when you've decided what
20   you're doing. *(Closes his eyes and leans back.)*
21 BEN: Yeah, me too.
22 BLAIR: *(Suddenly bored)* This party does sound pretty lame.
23 TAYLOR: Of course it does! We haven't decided on one thing
24   yet!
25 NADIA: Come on, Taylor, let's do it ourselves.
26 BLAIR: Wait a minute! What about Ebonee and me?
27 TAYLOR: *(Sadly)* Looks like girls outnumber boys again.
28 BEN: *(Satisfied)* Just the way I planned it.
29 ZECHARIAH: Yeah. Let the girls and Taylor do the work. We
30   can show up — that will be our part. *(Everyone exits*
31   *except MILAN.)*
32 MILAN: Sometimes when dealing with inferior personalities,
33   it doesn't pay to be too logical.

26. Do You Believe?

Topic: Twelve-year-olds discuss the age-old mystery of Santa Claus.

Cast:

RONI: a little hard-edged, worldly
TERRY: old for her age, world-wise
LONI: the last kid her age to learn the "truth"

1   *(Scene begins as ACTORS are sitting around on a sofa, or*
2   *playing video games.)*
3   RONI: Hey, Terry, what are your parents getting you for
4   Christmas?
5   TERRY: I asked for a computer and TV for my room. I'll
6   probably get clothes and junk I didn't ask for.
7   LONI: *(Sincerely)* What about Santa Claus?
8   TERRY: *(Clearly not having heard correctly)* Huh?
9   LONI: Well, did you ask Santa Claus for anything?
10 RONI: *(A little concerned)* Are you feeling OK, Loni?
11 LONI: Sure. Why?
12 RONI: Did you say "ask Santa Claus"?
13 LONI: Yes, of course.
14 TERRY: *(Suspiciously)* Did you ask Santa Claus for anything,
15   Loni?
16 LONI: Absolutely. I always ask for things and I get what I
17   want. Within reason, of course.
18 TERRY: *(Beginning to become worried about her friend)* Let me
19   get this straight. You actually go to the mall and sit on
20   that guy with the beard's lap and read from your goody
21   list?
22 LONI: Of course not.
23 RONI: Thank heavens.
24 LONI: *(Reasonably)* I write him a letter.
25 TERRY: *(Appalled)* You've got to be kidding.

1 LONI: Every year on Thanksgiving night I sit down and write
2   a very polite and grateful letter to Santa Claus. I've done
3   it since I was little and it works perfectly.
4 RONI: *(Very sincerely concerned)* Loni, please tell me you're
5   kidding. Please tell me you don't believe in Santa Claus.
6 LONI: Of course I believe in him. Don't you?
7 TERRY: Uh, *no.*
8 LONI: Roni?
9 RONI: I can't believe you're even asking.
10 LONI: *(A little saddened by her friends)* When did you become
11   disillusioned, Terry?
12 TERRY: What?
13 LONI: When did you stop believing?
14 TERRY: When I was like five. I saw my mom sticking the
15   gifts under the tree late at night.
16 LONI: And you, Roni?
17 RONI: I actually saw my dad eat half a cookie on Santa's
18   plate and put crumbs on the plate so it looked authentic.
19   I was seven.
20 LONI: *(Like a lawyer presenting evidence)* So, because of that
21   circumstantial evidence, you gave up believing in Santa
22   Claus?
23 TERRY: Come on, Loni, everyone knows there's no such
24   person.
25 LONI: Not everyone. I believe in him.
26 RONI: *(Exasperated)* I can't believe we're even having this
27   conversation.
28 LONI: Did you ever ask your parents about it?
29 TERRY: Sure, and they told me I was right. You need to take
30   a little reality trip, Loni, and grow up a little.
31 RONI: Yeah, it must be embarrassing to go around saying
32   things like that. I wouldn't tell the kids at school if I were
33   you. They'll tease you to death.
34 LONI: *(Slyly)* What if I'm right?
35 TERRY: You're not.

1 LONI: *(Insisting)* **What if I am?**
2 RONI: Loni, we're trying to tell you there's no such thing as
3   Santa. How did you get to be twelve without finding that
4   out?
5 LONI: *(Persistent and emphatic)* **What if you're wrong?**
6 RONI: Huh?
7 LONI: What if there is a Santa and, because you say he
8   doesn't exist, he doesn't come to your house?
9 TERRY: That's impossible.
10 LONI: Why? Didn't you get more presents when you believed
11   in him?
12 RONI: No. Not possible. I didn't ... *(Pauses and thinks a*
13   *minute)* well, it just seemed like I got more presents
14   because I was little. When you're five, a box of crayons
15   is a big deal. My mom could wrap up underwear and I
16   thought it was cool. She can't get away with that any
17   more.
18 LONI: Maybe you did get more presents.
19 TERRY: Only because kid toys cost like ten dollars and the
20   sweatshirt I want costs forty-eight dollars. We get less
21   now because our gifts are more expensive.
22 LONI: Maybe so. Maybe not.
23 RONI: You're going to try to keep on believing, in spite of
24   what we've told you and what everyone in the world
25   says?
26 LONI: Not everyone. There are lots of people who believe.
27   The spirit of Christmas is about faith and hope and
28   believing in something bigger than yourself. Maybe
29   everybody, even adults, would be happier if they believed
30   in a little magic.
31 TERRY: I can just see my dad sitting with a beer waiting up
32   all night for Santa to arrive and bring him that electric
33   drill my mom won't get him.
34 LONI: Maybe he'll get it this year.
35 TERRY: Maybe *I* should get it for him.

1   RONI: It would be fun to *play* Santa, though. To buy a couple
2   of things for my sisters and put them under the tree with
3   Santa on the tag and not tell them who it's from.
4   LONI: I see Santa is going to show up at your house this
5   year.
6   TERRY: I still think you're crazy, Loni, but it does sound like
7   fun.
8   LONI: Isn't that what it's all about?

27. How May I Help You?

Topic: Communication problems via the phone between an innocent citizen and corporate America.

Cast:
REP: almost mechanical, working on automatic pilot with not much emotion
CUSTOMER: trying painfully to bring a little logic to the conversation

1 *(This scene should take place with both ACTORS On-Stage.*
2 *Customer REP should be sitting at a desk with a headset to*
3 *serve as the phone and something to serve as a computer.*
4 *CUSTOMER should have a cell or regular phone. They should*
5 *be on opposite sides of the stage and never make eye*
6 *contact.)*
7 REP: *(Very rehearsed, professional, falsely cheerful)* **Hello, this is**
8   **National Credit Agency. How may I help you?**
9 CUSTOMER: **Hi. I'm calling to let you know my grandmother**
10   **has passed away and to cancel her account.**
11 REP: **OK. Could I please get the account number?**
12 CUSTOMER: *(Consulting a paper)* **Yes, that's five-six-nine-**
13   **one-two-five-four-six-seven.**
14 REP: **Thank you.** *(Clicks some keys on the computer. Consults*
15   *screen.)* **Yes, I see the account here. There is a three**
16   **hundred dollar balance.**
17 CUSTOMER: **Well, she died three months ago, in**
18   **September, and there was a zero dollar balance at that**
19   **time.**
20 REP: **Well, these charges are for annual fees and late**
21   **charges. There are also some penalties added for**
22   **October and November.**
23 CUSTOMER: **I just told you that she died in September.**
24 REP: **I understand, but she is still responsible for the late**
25   **charges and the fees.**

1 CUSTOMER: For fees and charges that were applied after
2   she died?
3 REP: *(Very logically)* The account wasn't cancelled.
4 CUSTOMER: *(A little confused)* But she died.
5 REP: Yes, I understand that. But the fees and late charges
6   are still due.
7 CUSTOMER: Let me get this clear. You are trying to collect
8   three hundred dollars from a dead woman who didn't buy
9   anything?
10 REP: *(Beginning to be bored)* If you have a copy of your
11   contract, you'll see where these fees and late charges
12   still apply unless an account is cancelled.
13 CUSTOMER: *(Speaking a little more slowly and clearly.*
14   *Obviously starting to get angry.)* I hope you heard me say
15   that this was my grandmother's account and that she is
16   *dead.* I don't have any contract.
17 REP: *(Unconcerned)* Well, it was mailed out with your original
18   credit card.
19 CUSTOMER: *(Surrendering)* You know what? Go ahead and
20   keep mounting up those fees and late charges. I'm sure
21   she won't mind.
22 REP: We advise our customers to keep up-to-date with their
23   bill. You really don't want to ruin her credit rating.
24 CUSTOMER: *(With a sudden idea)* How about this — would
25   you like her new address?
26 REP: That would very helpful, thank you.
27 CUSTOMER: The address is Saint Andrew Cemetery, Ten
28   Main Street.
29 REP: A cemetery? Her new address is at a cemetery?
30 CUSTOMER: Yes it is. Where do you bury people on your
31   planet?

28. The Principal's Office

Topic: A student is called to the principal's office — for a *good* reason.

Cast:
MRS. JEFFERSON: the typical principal, business-like but kind
ANDY: a kid with a guilty conscience

1　*(Scene should open with MRS. JEFFERSON sitting behind a*
2　*desk and ANDY sitting in a chair on the other side, obviously*
3　*uncomfortable.)*
4　**MRS. JEFFERSON: Well, Andy, I guess you know why I've**
5　**called you down to my office.**
6　**ANDY:** *(Trying to express regret)* **Yes, ma'am. I'm really sorry**
7　**about the problem on the basketball court.**
8　**MRS. JEFFERSON:** *(Confused)* **The problem on the**
9　**basketball court? I don't know about that, but maybe I**
10　**should. Want to tell me?**
11　**ANDY: No, ma'am. I mean, if you don't know, it's not**
12　**important. I mean, I don't want to bother you with it. I**
13　**mean, what was it you wanted?**
14　**MRS. JEFFERSON: It's interesting, Andy, that you've been**
15　**a student here for three years and I've never had you**
16　**down to my office.**
17　**ANDY: Yes, ma'am. That's a good thing, isn't it?**
18　**MRS. JEFFERSON: Yes, of course. How do you like it here**
19　**at Lincoln Middle?**
20　**ANDY:** *(Enthusiastically)* **Oh, it's great. I like it a lot.**
21　**MRS. JEFFERSON: The teachers and the other kids treat**
22　**you well?**
23　**ANDY: Yes, ma'am.**
24　**MRS. JEFFERSON: How about homework?** *(Consults a pad*
25　*or book.)* **I see here your grades are fine.**
26　**ANDY: A little bit too much homework sometimes, but not**
27　**too bad.**

1   MRS. JEFFERSON: Are you involved in any extracurricular
2   activities, Andy? Music lessons, sports, anything like
3   that?
4   ANDY: Ummmm ... well, I play basketball and I used to take
5   guitar lessons but I hated it, so I stopped.
6   MRS. JEFFERSON: Everything OK at home?
7   ANDY: What?
8   MRS. JEFFERSON: Your family. Everything OK with your
9   family?
10 ANDY: Sure. I mean, I guess so. My little sister's a pain in
11   the ... neck, but everything else is OK.
12 MRS. JEFFERSON: Well, that's their jobs, little sisters. I
13   wanted to talk to you about the Barrington Honor
14   Society. Have you heard of that?
15 ANDY: No, should I?
16 MRS. JEFFERSON: We usually reserve this for the high
17   school students, but I'm feeling led to talk to you about
18   it, Andy. Every year we send six students to Nicaragua
19   in an exchange program. They send students here to our
20   school. Have you met those students here at Lincoln?
21 ANDY: Do you mean Isabel and José? Sure, I've seen them
22   around.
23 MRS. JEFFERSON: Right, Isabel and José are both a part
24   of the program. Anyway, we send six students from our
25   school to Nicaragua and they send six of their students
26   here. They live in a college dormitory and meet the
27   people from the countries and, well, just get to share
28   themselves. It's a wonderful opportunity.
29 ANDY: *(Interested)* It sounds really cool.
30 MRS. JEFFERSON: Do you think you'd be interested in
31   participating in that program next year, Andy?
32 ANDY: *(Shocked)* What?
33 MRS.JEFFERSON: Would you like to join the Barrington
34   Honor Society and travel to Nicaragua with our team
35   next summer?

1   ANDY: *(Truly confused)* Why me? I'm not very smart and the
2   only Spanish I know is *Taco Bell*. I'm nobody special.
3   MRS. JEFFERSON: Well, I don't agree with that and neither
4   do your teachers. I know you're not the best student in
5   the eighth grade, but I think you're very smart. And you
6   are special. We think you'd be wonderful and make us
7   very proud over there. Willing to come to the meeting on
8   Friday to find out more?
9   ANDY: *(Enthusiastic and very pleased)* Sure! What do I have
10   to do?
11 MRS. JEFFERSON: Bring your parents and we'll talk Friday
12   after school. And, Andy, don't ever think you're not
13   special. I think you're *very* special. I hope you learn that
14   someday.

29. After School

Topic: A little darker skit that is open to interpretation by actors.

Cast:
ISAAC
BRENDA

This skit was specifically written to be ambiguous in meaning. It can be played several different ways. Try using the same actors and reading them with different interpretations. For instance, Isaac can be played as a stalker-type and Brenda is a typical girl. Or Isaac can be played as a normal guy and Brenda can be played as paranoid.

Suggestion
Pair up students and have them try both interpretations. Have them practice how the words themselves can be interpreted to change the meaning.

1 ISAAC: Hey, Brenda, what are you doing?

2 BRENDA: Nothing. Why?

3 ISAAC: Just asking. You walking home from school today?

4 BRENDA: Uh, no. My mom's coming.

5 ISAAC: You should walk home. You don't live far. You could
6   stop at like the 7-Eleven or something and get a snack.
7   It's cool. I do it all the time.

8 BRENDA: You know where I live?

9 ISAAC: Sure, it's on the bathroom wall. I'm just kidding. I
10   used to play ball at that school by your house and
11   somebody told me where you lived.

12 BRENDA: Well, I don't like to walk. I'm waiting for my mom.

13 ISAAC: She still got that beat-up Volkswagen?

14 BRENDA: You know what kind of car my mom drives?

15 ISAAC: Sure, I'm an observant guy.

16 BRENDA: I guess.

17 ISAAC: You don't like me, do you?

1   BRENDA: What do you mean?

2   ISAAC: You're not very nice to me.

3   BRENDA: I am too.

4   ISAAC: I know you and your friends talk about me, about

5   how I take dance and like to draw. I've seen you guys

6   laughing in the hall.

7   BRENDA: We don't talk about you. I don't laugh at you.

8   ISAAC: Yeah, right. Well, don't underestimate me, Brenda.

9   I'm a lot stronger than I look.

10 BRENDA: What's that supposed to mean?

11 ISAAC: You'll find out.

30. The Test

Topic: A play about cheating on a test.

Cast:
SAMI: a shady kid of questionable character
LEE: honest, forthright
JOE: appalled and angry by Sami's cheating

1   (Scene opens with SAMI joining LEE and JOE, who are
2   already standing Center Stage.)
3 SAMI: Hi, Lee. How ya been?
4 LEE: Fine. How about you?
5 SAMI: OK. What did you get on that science test today?
6 LEE: (Pleased) I got an eighty-five.
7 JOE: (Pitifully) I got a sixty. My mom's gonna kill me.
8 LEE: What did you get, Sami?
9 SAMI: (Very proudly) I got a hundred.
10 LEE and JO: (Shocked) What?
11 SAMI: (Innocently) What what? I scored and you two
12   bombed.
13 JOE: (Totally perplexed) How in the world did you get a
14   hundred? That was the hardest test I ever took.
15 LEE: (Also confused) I studied for like a week for that test.
16   How did you get a hundred?
17 SAMI: You make it sound like I'm stupid or something.
18 JOE: I didn't say that but ... well, yeah, you've never gotten
19   a hundred on anything in your life.
20 SAMI: That's not true. I get a hundred on every gym quiz we
21   have.
22 LEE: (Suddenly suspicious) Sami, you didn't cheat, did you?
23 SAMI: That's a mean thing to say, Lee.
24 JOE: (Realizing he's right) I can't believe it. You cheated off
25   of Jennifer Winslow, didn't you? That's why you kicked

1   Mario out of that seat, so you could sit next to Jennifer.
2   You totally cheated and I'm gonna tell.
3 SAMI: You're such a loser, Joe. You're just bummed out
4   because I aced it and you didn't.
5 LEE: Man, I can't believe you cheated.
6 SAMI: *(Irritated)* Shut up, Lee. You don't know what you're
7   talking about. Why are you guys all over my case? It's
8   just a stupid science test.
9 LEE: That's not the point. Cheating's wrong and you know
10   it. If Mr. Conner found out he'd kick you out of school.
11 SAMI: *(Menacing)* You tell him and I'll kick *you* — and not
12   out of school.
13 JOE: Knock it off, Sami. If you don't fess up, I'm gonna do
14   it for you. It's not fair to the rest of us that you'll be the
15   only one who gets a good grade.
16 SAMI: I'm not the *only* one. *(Slyly)* I heard Jennifer Winslow
17   did real well, too.
18 LEE: You're a jerk, Sami. There are more important things
19   in life than passing a test, you know.
20 SAMI: Like what?
21 LEE: Like honesty and truthfulness. But you wouldn't know
22   anything about that, would you?
23 JOE: Come on, Lee, let's go hang out with the other kids.
24   You know, the ones we can trust.
25 LEE: Right. And Sami, if you ever decide to join the human
26   race again, give us a call. *(They exit leaving SAMI alone.)*

31. Best Friends

Topic: Two friends battle out everyday problems.

Cast:
MARIA: a drama queen, overreacts, energetic
COURTNEY: Maria's well-meaning friend

1   *(Scene begins as MARIA comes On-Stage and storms up to*
2   *COURTNEY.)*
3 MARIA: Courtney Johnson, I'm never speaking to you for
4   the rest of my life. *(Turns her back and crosses her arms.)*
5 COUTNEY: What's wrong, Maria?
6 MARIA: I can't tell you because I'm not speaking to you.
7 COURTNEY: Are you mad about Conner?
8 MARIA: *(Turns back to COURTNEY. Suspicious)* What about
9   Conner?
10 COURTNEY: *(Imploringly, with hands up)* I swear I didn't kiss
11   him, no matter what those girls at the mall said. I know
12   he's your boyfriend and I wouldn't do that.
13 MARIA: *(Horrified)* You kissed my boyfriend?
14 COURTNEY: No, no, I swear I didn't.
15 MARIA: That wasn't what I was mad about, but now I am.
16 COURTNEY: Is it about the sweater?
17 MARIA: *(Suspicious again)* What sweater?
18 COURTNEY: I only borrowed it, I swear. I was going to
19   return it as soon as my Mom washed it. I got a little
20   pizza on it.
21 MARIA: My good cashmere sweater? You took my good
22   sweater and got pizza on it?
23 COURTNEY: I'll have it back Friday. Saturday at the latest,
24   I promise.
25 MARIA: I can't believe this. No, I wasn't mad about that
26   either, but the list is growing.

1　COURTNEY: *(Giving up and deciding to come completely clean)*
2　　OK. I'm really sorry I asked Mrs. Mantler to put me into
3　　a different study group in English, but I thought it would
4　　be better for all of us.
5　MARIA: You're the one who asked Mrs. Mantler to go to a
6　　different group? Why?
7　COURTNEY: *(Trying to make her understand)* It's just that
8　　when we study, sometimes you chew your gum really
9　　loud and it's really hard for me to concentrate. I didn't
10　mean anything by it, really. I bet Lizzy is a great study
11　partner, isn't she?
12　MARIA: So let me get this straight. You kissed my
13　　boyfriend, stole my best sweater, and got out of my
14　　study group in English. Anything else I should know?
15　COURTNEY: Isn't that enough?
16　MARIA: You would *think so,* but even *that's* not why I'm
17　　mad at you.
18　COURTNEY: You mean there's more?
19　MARIA: You tell me. What else should I know?
20　COURTNEY: OK, here it goes: *(Deep breath)* I was the one
21　　who broke your Barbie in the second grade. I was the
22　　one who told your mom you snuck out to meet Jimmy
23　　Smith last year. I accidentally told just a couple of
24　　people about your thumb-sucking. I'm the one that told
25　　Mr. Peters that you could sing and that's why you had
26　　to do that karaoke thing last year at the assembly. And
27　　... OK, I'm the one who's been writing those anonymous
28　　love letters to your brother. *(Pauses. Pitiful, eyes downcast)*
29　　You must hate me now. *(MARIA starts laughing.*
30　　*Completely confused)* What in the world are you laughing
31　　at? Aren't you furious with me?
32　MARIA: Well, that was a lot of bad stuff. But anyone who
33　　could have such a pathetic crush on my disgusting
34　　brother needs all the sympathy she can get.

32. The Dance

Topic: Two platonic friends discuss dates for a school dance.

Cast:
BOB: regular guy, a little clueless, not really getting the vibes Mary is sending
MARY: secretly likes Bob, trying to figure out how to let him know

1   *(Scene opens with both Center Stage.)*
2   **BOB:** Hey, Mary, you're not going to the dance Friday night,
3   are you?
4   **MARY:** *(Sarcastically)* I'm fine, Bob, how are you?
5   **BOB:** I mean it, man. I'm trying to find out who's going
6   Friday.
7   **MARIA:** Why?
8   **BOB:** Because I heard Donny Fondo is going with Susan
9   Miller and I need to know if it's true before I ask you.
10   **MARY:** What are you talking about?
11   **BOB:** I was going to ask Susan, but I heard she's already
12   going with Donny. If she is, I can't go by myself, so I was
13   going to ask you.
14   **MARY:** *(Offended and slightly sarcastic)* You were going to ask
15   me to go to the dance with you, but only after you were
16   sure the person you really wanted to go with was already
17   taken?
18   **BOB:** Right. Exactly.
19   **MARY:** *(Angry)* You're an idiot, Bob. I wouldn't go with you
20   if you were the last guy on earth.
21   **BOB:** What? Why?
22   **MARY:** *(Just to be mean)* And I heard that Susan Miller is
23   madly in love with Donny Fondo and wouldn't go out
24   with you in a million years.
25   **BOB:** Where did you hear that?

1 MARY: Honestly, Bob, you used to be a nice guy. What
2   happened?
3 BOB: I was never a nice guy, but that's not the point. Is it
4   true about Susan and Donny?
5 MARY: *(Exasperated)* Oh, I don't know! I just made that up
6   to make you mad.
7 BOB: *(Really clueless)* Why would you want to make me
8   mad? Are you having a bad day or something?
9 MARY: No, Bob, I'm not having a bad day. It's just that,
10   well, I *just* found out that this guy I really like likes
11   someone else.
12 BOB: No way.
13 MARY: Yeah, and he is going to ask me to the dance Friday
14   night as a backup because the girl he really likes is
15   going with someone else.
16 BOB: That's a really mean thing to do. You shouldn't go
17   with him.
18 MARY: *(She agrees, but he's utterly clueless.)* You're absolutely
19   right. Goodbye, Bob. *(She begins to exit.)*
20 BOB: *(He chases after her.)* Hey, Mary! What about Friday
21   night? Do you want to go to the dance?

33. He Said/She Said

Topic: Friends are confronted by the principal and need to clear up a mishap.

Cast:
MR. THOMPSON: principal
BRIAN
ALICE

1   *(Scene begins with MR. THOMPSON sitting behind desk and*
2   *BRIAN and ALICE entering together.)*
3   **BRIAN:** *(Cautiously)* **You wanted to see us, Mr. Thompson?**
4   **MR. THOMPSON: Yes. Please have a seat.** *(Both sit.)*
5   **ALICE: Are we in trouble?**
6   **MR. THOMPSON: I wanted to talk to you about the incident**
7   **with Steven Wilson.**
8   **BRIAN:** *(Puts his head in his hands.)* **Oh, no.**
9   **ALICE:** *(Hands up defensively.)* **I had nothing to do with it. I**
10   **swear, Mr. Thompson, it wasn't me.**
11   **BRIAN:** *(Looks angrily at her.)* **You're such a liar, Alice.**
12   **MR. THOMPSON: All right, all right, everybody calm down.**
13   **ALICE:** *(Pleading)* **My mom will kill me if I get in trouble**
14   **again.**
15   **MR. THOMPSON: I didn't say you were in trouble.**
16   **BRIAN: We wouldn't be here if we weren't.**
17   **MR. THOMPSON: Maybe you would like to tell me, in your**
18   **own words, what happened.**
19   **BRIAN:** *(Emphatic)* **Me first.**
20   **MR. THOMPSON: OK, go ahead, Brian.**
21   **BRIAN: OK, it was last Tuesday after school —**
22   **ALICE:** *(Interrupting)* **It was Wednesday.**
23   **BRIAN: No, it was Tuesday because I have lacrosse on**
24   **Tuesday nights.**

1 ALICE: It was Wednesday because I was late for
2   cheerleading.
3 MR. THOMPSON: *(Trying to move the conversation along)*
4   *Anyway* ...
5 BRIAN: OK, last *Tuesday* after school a couple of us were
6   walking home.
7 MR. THOMPSON: Who was walking with you?
8 BRIAN: Jason Turner, Michelle Moran, Jilly McKay, Stevey,
9   Alice, and me.
10 ALICE: Michelle wasn't there.
11 BRIAN: Yes, she was.
12 ALICE: No, she wasn't. I called her when I got home.
13 BRIAN: Yes, she was, because I borrowed a dollar from her
14   for the 7-Eleven.
15 MR. THOMPSON: *(Peacemaking)* OK, OK, we'll settle some
16   of these details later.
17 BRIAN: OK, we were walking up Center Avenue —
18 ALICE: We were on Oak Street.
19 BRIAN: And it was about four-thirty —
20 ALICE: It wasn't even four o'clock yet.
21 BRIAN: We saw this little boy —
22 ALICE: It was a girl.
23 BRIAN: *(Same time as ALICE)* Stevey said we should try to
24   take his ball and Alice and me started to go in the other
25   direction so we wouldn't get in trouble ...
26 ALICE: *(Same time as BRIAN)* Jason Turner started picking
27   on this little girl on a bike and Steve walked up to get in
28   between Jason and her ...
29 MR. THOMPSON: *(Stands up and holds out hands.)* Stop!
30   *(Pause)* Perhaps we'd make more progress if I
31   interviewed you individually? *Before* you have a chance to
32   corroborate your stories. You do know what corroborate
33   means, don't you?
34 BRIAN and ALICE: Invent?
35 MR. THOMPSON: Not exactly. Let's all take a nice walk and

1   find the vice principal. We'll get to the bottom of this.
2 **BRIAN:** *(To ALICE quietly)* **If only you could learn to be as**
3   **quiet in here as you are in science class.**
4 **ALICE:** *(To BRIAN)* **If only you were creative in writing class**
5   **as you are when you're making up stories.**

34. No Trespassing

Topic: An old, grumpy man makes friends with a student.

Cast:

MR. W: grouchy, burned-out, short-tempered, frustrated old man
NICK: defensive, but basically a good kid

1   *(Scene begins with MR. W slowly chasing after NICK, who is*
2   *crossing the stage.)*
3   **MR. W: Hey you, kid. Come here a minute.**
4   **NICK:** *(Wary)* **Yeah?**
5   **MR. W:** *Yeah?* **Don't you have no manners?**
6   **NICK:** *(Not interested in being friendly)* **Do you need**
7   **something?**
8   **MR. W: I just want to know what the heck you think you are**
9   **doing trespassing on my lawn.**
10 **NICK: I didn't trespass on your lawn.**
11 **MR. W:** *(Waving hands, pointing finger)* **Don't tell me you**
12   **didn't. I saw you. Yesterday afternoon you and your**
13   **friends were playing ball and went and hit it over my**
14   **fence. Climbed right over the fence and into my yard you**
15   **come. Don't say you didn't do it.**
16 **NICK:** *(Remembering, then getting caught up in the story)* **I'm**
17   **sorry, I didn't mean to trespass. We never hit it that far**
18   **before. That Jimmy Washington has a real good bat and**
19   **he just ripped one. I won't go on your lawn anymore.**
20 **MR. W: Back in my days we knew how to respect people's**
21   **property. Never walk on a neighbor's yard without first**
22   **asking.**
23 **NICK: You're right. I should have knocked on your door and**
24   **asked first.**
25 **MR. W:** *(Backing down a little)* **Well, don't go knocking on my**
26   **door during** *The Price is Right.* **I'd get really mad about**

1   that. No, it's all right, just don't trip on that trash back
2   there and break a leg and go and sue me. Can't afford
3   no lawsuit, that's for sure.
4 NICK: Yeah, uh, I noticed that trash. *(Hesitant to suggest)*
5   Would you like, I mean, I'd be happy to help clear some
6   of that trash out for you. Looks like you had some
7   remodeling done. I could put it out front on trash day if
8   you'd like.
9 MR. W: Doggone workers, charge me an arm and a leg to fix
10   the floor in my kitchen and then leave a huge truckload
11   of trash in the backyard. Don't haul it away, don't
12   apologize. Nobody apologizes. Nobody cares an old man
13   has arthritis and a bum knee and can't carry that trash
14   around.
15 NICK: Really, I'd be happy to clear it out for you.
16 MR. W: *(Dismissively, defensively)* I can't afford no helper.
17 NICK: I wouldn't charge you. I don't mind. It won't take me
18   more than a couple of minutes. In fact, I'll bet my friends
19   will be glad to help me and we can get it all cleared out
20   in no time at all.
21 MR. W: *(Becoming suspicious)* Why would you do that?
22 NICK: *(Shrugging, innocent)* I don't know. I don't mind doing
23   it. It will only take a couple of minutes.
24 MR. W: *(Apparently not accustomed to kindness from kids)* I
25   don't know what to say.
26 NICK: It's all right. You don't have to say anything. We'll
27   come over on Wednesday night after dinner and put it
28   out for the trash. No problem.
29 MR. W: *(Now friendly and eager to chat)* Well, that's really nice
30   of you young man. I think I have cookies sitting around
31   that I can get out. I might even put my lawn chair out
32   front and watch your game. Planning on playing baseball
33   on Wednesday night?
34 NICK: I don't know. Maybe. If it's not raining.
35 MR. W: All right then. I might even have some pointers for

1   you. I was quite the ball player in my day. Never
2   trespassed on an old man's lawn, but I got a hold of a
3   long one or two in my day.
4 **NICK:** Cool. See ya then. *(Exits.)*

35. Happy Halloween

Topic: Opening communication between generations on a favorite holiday

Cast:
LADY: sweet, kind, chatty old lady
SAM: impatient, insensitive
BRIAN: a little more sympathetic and willing to placate the old lady

1 *(Scene opens as LADY is opening door to BRIAN and SAM.)*
2 **BRIAN and SAM: Trick or treat.**
3 **LADY:** *(Enthusiastically)* **Oh, look at the cute little kids.**
4 **Father, come look. We have two scary trick-or-treaters.**
5 **SAM:** *(To BRIAN)* **Good grief. This is getting old.**
6 **BRIAN: Come on, Sam, deal with it. These old people give**
7 **out the best candy.**
8 **LADY:** *(To BRIAN)* **And what are *you* supposed to be, young**
9 **man?**
10 **BRIAN:** *(Accommodatingly)* **I'm a hobo.**
11 **LADY: Ooooh, a hobo, how sweet.** *(To SAM)* **And you?**
12 **SAM:** *(Sarcastically, not particularly friendly)* **Hello? I'm a**
13 **mummy. Bandages, get it?**
14 **LADY: I see, yes, I see. Father, are you coming? I want you**
15 **to see these scary children. Now, do you two live in the**
16 **neighborhood?**
17 **BRIAN: Yeah, down on Maypole Court.**
18 **LADY: Oh yes, Maypole Court. I used to play bridge with**
19 **Mariann Clement who lived on Maypole. Do you know**
20 **her?**
21 **SAM:** *(Impatiently)* **No. We gotta go.**
22 **BRIAN:** *(Quietly to SAM)* **Man, get a grip.** *(To LADY)* **We just**
23 **moved in a few months ago and we don't know many**
24 **people on the street. Only people with kids.**

1   LADY: Well, I'll bet Mariann's grandchildren come to visit
2   some times. I'll bet you'll meet them eventually. I'm sure
3   she'd be happy to know you. Why don't you stop by and
4   introduce yourself?
5   SAM: *(Sarcastically)* Gee, Brian, I think I heard Mommy
6   calling. We'd better take off. Bye now.
7   BRIAN: To be honest, ma'am, the older people on the street
8   are kind of mean to us. They don't let us play basketball
9   in the street and yell if we ride our skateboards after six
10   because they say the noise keeps them up.
11 LADY: Oh, dear, I see. Yes, it is hard for some older people
12   to remember what it was like when they were
13   youngsters. I remember when I was your age ...
14 SAM: *(Rolling eyes)* Good grief.
15 LADY: There was a mean old lady at the bottom of our
16   street named Mrs. Bond, but we just called her the cat
17   lady because she seemed to have about one hundred
18   cats. If we so much as walked on her lawn she'd come
19   after us with a broom. One time she called the police
20   because we were sitting across the street on the steps
21   of the dime store talking. *(Sigh)* It's very hard to get old,
22   you know.
23 BRIAN: Do you ... do you have children?
24 LADY: Oh, yes, we have sixteen living children.
25 SAM: *(Shocked)* Sixteen?
26 BRIAN: *(Confused)* Living?
27 LADY: Yes, we lost a daughter when she was just a baby.
28   Such a tragedy. But the good Lord has given us many
29   blessings and forty-seven grandchildren. Wait, I think it's
30   forty-eight. Yes, forty-eight. Time does catch up with us.
31 SAM: Wow. Do they all fit into your house at one time?
32 LADY: *(Laughs.)* We have had them all here, but mostly we
33   go to my son's house in Bentley. He's a doctor and lives
34   in quite a big house. But, well, I'm sure you want to get
35   on with your trick-or-treating and don't want to waste

1   time with an old lady like me.
2 SAM: *(Kindly)* It's OK. It's kind of cool hearing about that
3   stuff.
4 LADY: Well, aren't you sweet? Here's your treats. In fact, I
5   think I'll give you these extra large treats we keep for the
6   grandchildren. You have been so sweet. I don't know
7   what happened to Father. I wanted him to meet you.
8   Well, please tell Mariann Clement I said hello.
9 BRIAN: Will do. We'll try to look her up. Have a good night.
10   And thanks!
11 LADY: Thanks to you, too, boys. Happy Halloween!

36. Trick or Treat

Topic: Two friends discuss differing views on Halloween costumes.

Cast:
MOLLY: a girly-girl
JENNY: a tomboy

1   *(Scene begins with both GIRLS sitting on sofa or bed looking*
2   *through magazines.)*
3 **MOLLY:** So, Jenny, what are you going to be for Halloween?
4 **JENNY:** I haven't decided yet. My grandmother was
5   supposed to be making me this really terrific vampire
6   costume, but she got sick and so now I don't have
7   anything to wear.
8 **MOLLY:** *(Helpfully)* I could lend you one of my old costumes.
9 **JENNY:** *(Hesitantly)* Uh, thanks, but no.
10 **MOLLY:** Why?
11 **JENNY:** I don't know how to tell you this, but ... well, Molly,
12   your costumes are pretty lame sometimes.
13 **MOLLY:** *(Defensively)* Lame? What are you talking about? I
14   always have the best costumes in class. I've won three
15   mall costume contests. How many have you won?
16 **JENNY:** Little Bo Peep? Belle from *Beauty and the Beast*?
17   Sure, they were pretty but, well, I'm twelve, Molly. I'm
18   not gonna be a fairy tale character for Halloween. So,
19   anyway, what are you gonna be?
20 **MOLLY:** *(Harrumphing)* I'm not telling you now. I'm mad at
21   you. Besides, you'll make fun of me.
22 **JENNY:** *(Sincerely)* I'm sorry. I won't. You always look really
23   ... pretty.
24 **MOLLY:** Sure, you're just saying that.
25 **JENNY:** No I'm not. I'm serious. Tell me what you're gonna be.
26 **MOLLY:** Well, I'm going to be a pirate.

1   JENNY: *(Excited)* That's cool! A real nasty one with a patch
2   and a sword and lots of blood?
3   MOLLY: No, the pretty one from *Pirates of the Caribbean*. You
4   know, Elizabeth. I have this beautiful long white dress
5   with a beautiful gold coin necklace and —
6   JENNY: I don't believe you. You aren't going to be a pirate.
7   You're going to be a princess.
8   MOLLY: She wasn't a princess, she was a pirate. At least
9   she was once she married that handsome Orlando
10   Bloom.
11 JENNY: You're absolutely hopeless. Don't you understand
12   that Halloween is supposed to be scary, nasty stuff with
13   blood and guts and ghosts and things like that?
14 MOLLY: It is not. You only think it is. It can be anything you
15   want it to be, and I like dressing up pretty. What's wrong
16   with that? When else am I going to be able to wear
17   something pretty like that?
18 JENNY: I guess you're right. I like the gross stuff. You know,
19   like the haunted houses, the bloody chainsaws, and the
20   scary music.
21 MOLLY: And I like the cute babies in pumpkin costumes and
22   the hayrides and all that candy.
23 JENNY: *(Eyes light up.)* Oh yeah, baby, the candy! Does it
24   really matter what we wear? As long as we get the
25   *candy!*
26 MOLLY: That's right. So you go ahead and be as gross as
27   you want and I'll be as pretty as I can, and I'll meet you
28   at six o'clock on Friday so we can go trick-or-treating.
29 JENNY: I only have one request.
30 MOLLY: What's that?
31 JENNY: Don't wear glass slippers or anything. Wear
32   comfortable shoes.
33 MOLLY: Why?
34 JENNY: So we can hit every house in the neighborhood that
35   has a light on the front porch!

37. The Band

Topic: Band members try to select a name for their band.

Cast:
ANN: the leader, full of energy
JASON: not real hopeful about the band's future
CHERI: trying to be helpful
TERRY: disillusioned
MIKE: comic relief

1　*(Scene opens with ALL sitting around. Musical instruments*
2　　*can be held or in view but are not audibly played during*
3　　*scene.)*
4　**ANN:** Come on, guys, we've got to pick a name for our band,
5　　like, yesterday.
6　**JASON:** What's the rush? It's not like we have a big music
7　　video to film or anything.
8　**CHERI:** Well, we might get one if we have a really cool name.
9　　Everyone knows how important the power of suggestion is.
10　**TERRY:** *(Discouraged)* Oh, give me a break. We can call
11　　ourselves Purple Snot and we wouldn't get a gig.
12　**MIKE:** *(Trying to lighten the mood)* Wait a minute, Purple
13　　Snot. I think that's a perfect name for the band.
14　**CHERI:** You've got to be kidding.
15　**JASON:** Of course he's kidding. I think that name's already
16　　taken, anyway.
17　**ANN:** *(Trying to be serious)* I think we should put some
18　　thought into this. What's a great band without a great
19　　name? Where would Black Sabbath be without such a
20　　terrific name like that?
21　**TERRY:** *(Not convinced)* I think that's a horrible name. It's
22　　the music that counts, not the name.
23　**MIKE:** I agree. Who cares what we call ourselves if our
24　　music is good?

1 CHERI: You guys are totally wrong. A name is super
2   important. Come on, give out some suggestions.
3 ANN: OK, here's one — Pastel Vibrations.
4 JASON: Good grief, what a girly name.
5 ANN: All right, smart aleck, you come up with one.
6 JASON: All right. OK, here's a great name — Dashing
7   Turtles.
8 MIKE: I like Pastel Vibrations better than Dashing Turtles.
9   Does that make any sense to anyone?
10 TERRY: There are some really bizarre names out there for
11   bands and things.
12 CHERI: Yeah, did you ever think about some of the names
13   for professional ball teams? Like Florida Marlins. That's
14   a fish. What's a fish got to do with baseball?
15 JASON: What's an oriole got to do with baseball or a raven
16   with football? It's supposed to represent a place, not tell
17   how good the team is. Otherwise they'd name their
18   teams like The New York Bad-Attitude-but-Rich-Team-
19   Winners.
20 ANN: Can we *please* get back to the band name? Who cares
21   about ball team names? We need suggestions for our
22   band. Come on, Terry, you're creative. Think of
23   something.
24 TERRY: How about the Green Hornets?
25 MIKE: Uh, taken. Don't you ever go to the movies?
26 TERRY: *(Throws hands up in frustration.)* Well, I don't know!
27 CHERI: All right, let's try to link the name to us personally.
28   We're all really cool, good-looking kids from Baltimore.
29   How about The Baltimore Blue Band?
30 MIKE: Where did *blue* come from?
31 CHERI: I don't know. It goes with *Baltimore* and *Band.*
32 ANN: You guys aren't even trying. Mike, come up with
33   something.
34 MIKE: All right. Cheri is right about linking it to us. How
35   about The Gifted Geeks?

1 JASON: Speak for yourself, geek. What an awful name.
2 ANN: We are getting nowhere. I guess we should all think
3   about it and try this again another time.
4 MIKE: You're right. We'll try again later. We have more
5   important things to decide right now anyway.
6 TERRY: Such as what?
7 MIKE: Have we decided which one of us is going to try to
8   learn to play an instrument?

38. Working It

Topic: Two friends try to figure out how to get around a mom.

Cast:
RYAN: the mastermind, expert on manipulation
BJ: a willing student of Ryan's

1   *(Scene begins with the two BOYS sitting or walking Center*
2   *Stage.)*
3   BJ: You go ask her.
4   RYAN: Why should I ask her?
5   BJ: She likes you better than she likes me.
6   RYAN: That's terrific. She's *your* mother.
7   BJ: I know. That's why she likes you better.
8   RYAN: Maybe, but she still yells at me.
9   BJ: Not as loud as she yells at me.
10 RYAN: All right, I'll ask her, but we have to formulate a plan.
11 BJ: A plan?
12 RYAN: Yeah. You just don't go up to a mom and ask her to
13   do something huge. You have to work out a plan.
14 BJ: All right. Any ideas?
15 RYAN: OK. Let's see. What has she been bugging you to do
16   lately?
17 BJ: The list is long and complex, my friend.
18 RYAN: Let's start with the most nagged-about thing.
19 BJ: My room.
20 RYAN: Yeah, it's always the room. Why do moms care so
21   much about our rooms?
22 BJ: Yeah, it's not like she ever has to go in there or
23   anything.
24 RYAN: Well, in your case, she probably fears for your life.
25 BJ: Oh, ha ha.
26 RYAN: So what particularly about your room is she upset with?

1 BJ: Have you seen my room?

2 RYAN: Good point. You know, it's really the effort they want
3   to see.

4 BJ: Huh?

5 RYAN: See, you don't really understand women like I do.

6 BJ: Oh, here we go.

7 RYAN: They don't really care what you *do*. It's that you
8   make some sort of attempt, even if it's a lame attempt.

9 BJ: So I don't have to really *do* anything, I just have to
10   attempt?

11 RYAN: Not exactly. You have to do *something*. Superficial
12   stuff, you know. Move some of the big stuff, throw out
13   the trash, you know. It will only take a few minutes to
14   make it look like you made a huge effort.

15 BJ: Oh, I get it. Just so she can see the rug.

16 RYAN: Right, now you're getting it. Clear off enough space
17   so that she can see the rug.

18 BJ: Oh, and the laundry.

19 RYAN: Great! Good idea. Ask her a question about her
20   laundry so that she thinks you're planning on doing
21   laundry. Don't ask for anything then, but just ask a
22   question about how much detergent to use or
23   something. That's a great touch.

24 BJ: Should I offer to cook dinner or something?

25 RYAN: Don't overdo it, BJ.

26 BJ: OK, got it. You really think she'll fall for this?

27 RYAN: Women, especially moms, are a sucker when they
28   see their kids "shaping up."

29 BJ: How long do I have to keep this up?

30 RYAN: Just as long as it takes to get her in a good mood,
31   and then you ask her.

32 BJ: Won't she get mad or figure it out?

33 RYAN: Sure, but what do you care? You'll already have what
34   you want.

35 BJ: You're a little scary, you know that?

36 RYAN: Yeah. Ain't it great?

39. Scary Teacher

Topic: Students dare to approach a teacher.

Cast:
JILLIAN: kind of bossy, a little afraid of the teacher
JULIA: timid, willing to work out a plan
CASSIE: logical and straightforward

1   *(Scene opens with the GIRLS Center Stage in a horseshoe*
2   *configuration playing rock, paper, scissors.)*
3   **JILLIAN: OK, go. Rock, paper, scissors!** *(They all choose*
4   *rock.)*
5   **JULIA: Let's do it again. Rock, paper, scissors!** *(They all*
6   *choose paper.)*
7   **CASSIE: We could be here all day doing this.**
8   **JILLIAN: It would be easier if one of us just volunteered to**
9   **do it.**
10 **CASSIE:** *(Grabbing this idea)* **Thanks, Jillian, that would be**
11   **great. Go ahead.**
12 **JILLIAN:** *(Sarcastically)* **Yeah, right. Let's go again. Rock,**
13   **paper —**
14 **JULIA: This is stupid. We should all go together.**
15 **CASSIE: I don't want to. You two can go.**
16 **JILLIAN: I don't want to. You two can go.**
17 **JULIA:** *(Trying to be reasonable)* **Come on, guys. I'll go if you**
18   **both come with me.** *(They pause.)*
19 **JILLIAN: No, I still don't want to go. She hates me. She'll**
20   **yell at me.**
21 **JULIA: She does not hate you.**
22 **CASSIE: Yeah, I think she's right. She does hate Jillian.**
23 **JULIA:** *(Frustrated)* **Oh, for goodness sake!**
24 **JILLIAN: She never picks me for messenger and last week**
25   **when I was late she made me take that math test.**

1 JULIA: We *all* took the math test.

2 JILLIAN: Yeah, but she put it on my desk real mean-like.

3 CASSIE: *(Trying to bring them back on task)* We're not really
4   getting anywhere with this. Why don't we just write a
5   note and leave it on her desk?

6 JULIA: That never works. Remember when she said adults
7   admire kids who speak up?

8 JILLIAN: Yeah, they always say that, until you actually *do*
9   speak up.

10 JULIA: We're just gonna have to ask her. Together. In
11   person.

12 CASSIE: Julia's right. She's just a human being, after all.
13   What can she do to us?

14 JILLIAN: Are you kidding? She's a *teacher*. She can do
15   anything she wants to us!

16 JULIA: Not true. She's not that bad. We just have to be
17   respectful-like. Let's practice.

18 JILLIAN: *(Suddenly excited)* Oh, let me be her, please?

19 CASSIE: Oh, OK.

20 JILLIAN: *(Gets snooty, acting like a grown-up.)* Yes, girls, is
21   there something you need?

22 JULIA: Uh, Miss Tambor, we'd like to speak to you a
23   minute.

24 JILLIAN: Fine, but make it quick. I'm late for my karate
25   lesson.

26 CASSIE: Jillian!

27 JILLIAN: Oh, OK. *(Changes back to modified grown-up.)* Yes,
28   girls, what is it?

29 CASSIE: Miss Tambor, we'd like to ask if you would
30   consider allowing us to have a bake sale.

31 JILLIAN: A bake sale? For what purpose?

32 JULIA: To raise money for our trip to New York.

33 JILLIAN: *(Short pause, pretending to consider)* All right. That
34   would be fine. *(They pause.)*

35 CASSIE: Well, that was kinda easy.

1   JULIA: Do you think it will be that easy with her?
2   JILLIAN: Only one way to find out. Let's go.
3   CASSIE: Hey, Jillian. Remember, you're not an adult
4   anymore.
5   JILLIAN: Right. I'll behave.
6   JULIA: Sure. I believe that. *(They exit.)*

40. Permanent Probation

Topic: A goofy driver is pulled over by an overworked police officer.

Cast:
OFFICER: trying to keep things going smoothly, very professional
DALE: completely clueless, should be nowhere near a moving vehicle

1 *(Scene can be set with DALE sitting in a chair pretending to*
2 *hold a steering wheel, facing forward. OFFICER approaches*
3 *from behind.)*
4 **OFFICER: Can I see your license and registration, please?**
5 **DALE: Why, officer? Was I speeding?**
6 **OFFICER: License and registration, please.**
7 **DALE:** *(Slight hesitation)* **Well, there might be a slight**
8 **problem with that.**
9 **OFFICER:** *(Steps back, speaks emphatically)* **Step out of the**
10 **car, please.**
11 **DALE: OK, OK.**
12 **OFFICER: What's the problem with the license and**
13 **registration?**
14 **DALE: Don't have it.**
15 **OFFICER: You mean you left your identification at home?**
16 **DALE: No, I mean I don't have it.**
17 **OFFICER: You don't have a license?**
18 **DALE: Do I look sixteen to you?**
19 **OFFICER: Exactly how old are you?**
20 **DALE: Can I go to jail for lying to a policeman?**
21 **OFFICER: Whose car is this?**
22 **DALE: My dad's.**
23 **OFFICER: Does he know you're driving without a license?**
24 **DALE: Of course not. Don't be silly. It was my *mom's* idea.**
25 **OFFICER: Do you have your learner's?**
26 **DALE: Don't you have to be like fifteen or something to get**
27 **that?**

1 OFFICER: What exactly are you doing driving without so
2   much as a learner's permit?
3 DALE: It was an emergency.
4 OFFICER: What type of emergency?
5 DALE: We ran out of chocolate chip cookie dough ice cream.
6 OFFICER: You consider *that* an emergency?
7 DALE: If you met my mom, you would understand.
8 OFFICER: I'm sure I will be meeting her very soon. Please
9   get into the rear seat of my vehicle.
10 DALE: You mean I get to ride in a cop car?
11 OFFICER: I need to take you down to the station and
12   contact your parents.
13 DALE: Can we stop to get the ice cream on the way?
14 OFFICER: You know what receiving a citation without a
15   license means, don't you?
16 DALE: That you can't suspend my license?
17 OFFICER: In a way, we can. Your probationary period has
18   just been extended three months.
19 DALE: You mean three *extra* months before I get my license?
20 OFFICER: That's exactly what I mean.
21 DALE: No jail time?
22 OFFICER: Not this time.
23 DALE: Well, that's good anyway. I hate to become a
24   hardened criminal before I turn thirteen.
25 OFFICER: You're well on your way. Let's go. *(They exit.)*

41. The Spelling Bee

Topic: A student gets ready for that all-too-familiar spelling bee.

Cast:
ADELLE: panicked, frightened, fidgeting
BRIANNA and EBONY: supportive, kind friends

1　*(Scene opens as ADELLE is pacing back and forth on the*
2　*stage. BRIANNA and EBONY are trying to keep her calm.)*
3　**ADELLE:** *(Whining)* **I look awful.**
4　**BRIANNA: You don't look awful.**
5　**EBONY: You look beautiful.**
6　**ADELLE:** *(Feeling her hair)* **My hair is sticking out like a rag**
7　　**doll's.**
8　**EBONY: It is not! Your hair looks fine.**
9　**ADELLE: I have a huge pimple on my forehead.**
10　**BRIANNA: No one will ever notice it.**
11　**ADELLE: Everyone will laugh at me.**
12　**BRIANNA:** *(Puts her hands on her shoulders.)* **Adelle, you have**
13　　**to calm down. No one will laugh at you.**
14　**EBONY: Stop worrying, Adelle. You're gonna do great.**
15　**ADELLE:** *(Mountingly nervous)* **You don't know that. I'm**
16　　**going to do terribly. I'm so nervous.**
17　**BRIANNA:** *(Trying to be convincing and comforting)* **Don't be**
18　　**nervous. Adelle, you won the spelling bee fair and**
19　　**square. You're going to beat every kid here.**
20　**ADELLE: I am not. I know I'm not. Did you see that girl from**
21　　**Georgia? She looks smart — you can tell.**
22　**EBONY: She does not. She looks even more nervous than**
23　　**you do.**
24　**BRIANNA: I think I saw her throwing up in the bathroom.**
25　**ADELLE: Don't give me any ideas! Did you see my mom?**
26　　**Where's my mom?! I can't go on without my mother!**

1 EBONY: *(Turning ADELLE to face her and leading her in the*
2   *breathing)* **Breathe, Adelle, deeeep, sloooow breaths.**
3   **She's sitting in her seat waiting for you to go on. They**
4   **wouldn't let her backstage, you know that.**
5 ADELLE: Oh, right. I forgot. I … forgot everything! How do
6   you spell *forgot?* I can't think of a single spelling word.
7   What am I doing here? I can't do this! I can't go out
8   there!
9 BRIANNA: *Adelle! Stop it right now! (Adelle takes a breath.)*
10   You've studied, you're smart, your hair looks terrific, and
11   you're going to do great. Take a deep breath. You'll do
12   well and make us all proud.
13 ADELLE: *(More calm)* **OK. You're right. I'm fine. I can do this.**
14   *I before E except after C.* I'll be fine. I've studied a lot and
15   I can do this.
16 EBONY: *(Happy to see she's calming down)* **That's the spirit,**
17   **Adelle!**
18 BRIANNA: That-a-girl! You're gonna be perfect.
19 ADELLE: *(Sincerely taking their hands)* **Thanks, guys. I**
20   **couldn't have done this without you.**
21 EBONY: Remember that when you're getting that five
22   hundred dollar prize. I'll take my part in cash, thank you
23   very much. *(They laugh. Suddenly they ALL look Off-stage.)*
24 BRIANNA: That girl from Georgia just messed up big time!
25   You're on!
26 ADELLE: I think I can … I think I can … I think I can … *(She*
27   *exits.)*
28 BRIANNA: She's gonna get creamed.
29 EBONY: Good thing she didn't see that boy from Texas.
30 BRIANNA: Let's go get a big box of Kleenex ready. She's
31   gonna need it! *(They exit.)*

42. Workin' 9 to 5

Topic: Kids discuss career options.

Cast:
CASEY: a wise, deep thinker
LINCOLN: smart, enthusiastic
BETSY: logical, smart
PAUL: has a very interesting idea about his future

1   *(Scene opens as ALL are sitting around doing homework.)*
2   CASEY: Ever thought of what you're gonna wanna do when
3   you grow up?
4   LINCOLN: I'm gonna be an engineer.
5   BETSY: I'm gonna be a doctor.
6   CASEY: I'm gonna be an astronaut.
7   PAUL: I'm gonna do nothing.
8   LINCOLN: What?
9   PAUL: I've been thinking about it a lot, and I think I'm not
10   gonna do anything.
11   BETSY: *(Suspiciously)* That's not a career choice.
12   PAUL: It could be.
13   CASEY: *(Disgusted)* Paul, that's the dumbest thing I ever
14   heard. No one grows up to be a nothing.
15   BETSY: Yeah. How are you gonna earn a living?
16   PAUL: *(Insightfully)* Well, the way I see it, you're all gonna
17   have six-figure jobs.
18   LINCOLN: What's a six-figure job?
19   PAUL: You know, where you earn hundreds of thousands of
20   dollars a year.
21   CASEY: That will be so cool.
22   BETSY: I want a huge house with a built-in swimming pool.
23   LINCOLN: I want to get my pilot's license and have my own
24   plane.
25   CASEY: I want to have a vacation home in Hawaii.

1 PAUL: Exactly right. You're all gonna have all those things.

2 BETSY: And what are *you* gonna have?

3 PAUL: Several very rich and *generous* friends who will let me
4   stay in their big houses, swim in their pools, fly in their
5   planes, and stay at their condo in Hawaii.

6 LINCOLN: *(Emphatically)* Forget it.

7 CASEY: He's right. You're not coming to my place in Hawaii.

8 PAUL: Well, why not?

9 BETSY: If you're too lazy to get a job and pay for your own
10   stuff, why should we let you use ours?

11 LINCOLN: Right.

12 PAUL: You mean I can't swim in your pool, Betsy?

13 BETSY: Not only can you not swim in my pool but, if you're
14   old like thirty or something and don't even have a job,
15   you won't even be able to visit. I don't want such a bad
16   influence on my twin girls, Chloe and Zoe.

17 CASEY: Yikes. Nice names.

18 LINCOLN: Besides, don't you want to *do* something?

19 PAUL: Sure I do. I want to swim in Betsy's pool —

20 LINCOLN: No, I mean, don't you want to make a difference
21   in the world?

22 BETSY: I want to be a doctor not just so I can make lots of
23   money, which I'll need for the horses for my girls, but I
24   want to help people, too.

25 LINCOLN: And my uncle's an engineer and he helps design
26   weapons for the military. Think of how cool that would
27   be.

28 CASEY: We need to find out if life can exist on other planets.
29   I plan on going to find out.

30 PAUL: Wow, you guys have put a lot of thought into this,
31   haven't you?

32 BETSY: A little, but my mom says it doesn't really matter
33   *what* you choose to do as long as you're happy and
34   you're helping people.

35 PAUL: You think we're all supposed to help people?

1   LINCOLN: Sure. Why else are we here?

2   CASEY: Yeah, what's the point if we don't make some sort

3   of a difference with our lives?

4   PAUL: I never thought about that. Maybe you're right. I

5   wonder what I could do.

6   BETSY: Clown.

7   LINCOLN: Garbage man.

8   CASEY: I hear McDonald's is always hiring.

9   PAUL: Sweet. I wonder if you can have all the fries you can

10   eat for free?

11 BETSY: *You* will put them right out of business.

43. Party Girls

Topic: Friends discuss whether to go to the "cool" party or not.

Cast:
KELSEY: enjoys fun, open to ideas
QUINCHE: the ultimate party girl, loves to fit in
MEGAN: more down-to-earth, less excited by the party life

1   *(Scene opens with KELSEY and QUINCHE Center Stage as*
2   *MEGAN joins them.)*
3   MEGAN: Hi, guys. What's up?
4   KELSEY: *(A little sad)* Hi, Megan. We're a little depressed.
5   MEGAN: Aw. Why?
6   QUINCHE: My mom won't let me go to Sierra's party.
7   MEGAN: Well, maybe that's not such a bad thing. I wasn't
8   going to go.
9   KELSEY: *(Surprised)* You're kidding! Why wouldn't you go?
10 MEGAN: I really didn't want to.
11 QUINCHE: You mean you weren't invited.
12 MEGAN: Oh, I was invited. But I'm not going.
13 QUINCHE: Why not? You must be nuts. Everybody who's
14   *anybody* is going to be there ... except for me.
15 KELSEY: *(Sadly)* Well, if you don't go, I don't have a ride, so
16   I guess I'm not going either.
17 MEGAN: I don't think you'll be missing much. Don't worry
18   about it.
19 KELSEY: Why?
20 MEGAN: Well, I heard her parties are pretty ... *(Hesitatingly)*
21   wild.
22 QUINCHE: I know! They're all anyone talks about! I *soooo*
23   wanted to go.
24 KELSEY: Really!
25 MEGAN: And her parents don't even stay home.

1   KELSEY: Exactly! Unchaperoned good times!

2   MEGAN: I don't think the *times* are all that fun.

3   KELSEY: *(Anxious for the gossip)* What have you heard?

4   MEGAN: Last spring someone had to call the police for one

5   of Sierra's parties.

6   QUINCHE: *(Excited by the prospect)* Awesome! That would be

7   so fun!

8   MEGAN: It's fun to be at a party that's so wild you have to

9   call in the police?

10   KELSEY: *(Rethinking)* Well ... maybe not so much fun.

11   QUINCHE: *(Whining)* I wanna goooo!

12   MEGAN: *(Suddenly inspired)* I've got a really good idea! What

13   if I ask my mom if you guys can come over to my house

14   and spend the night? We can rent a movie and eat junk

15   food all night!

16   KELSEY: That sounds really fun. Can you lock your little

17   brother up before we get there?

18   MEGAN: You've got a deal!

19   QUINCHE: I guess that would be better than staying home.

20   My mom *loves* your mom, so I'm sure she'll let me come

21   to your house.

22   KELSEY: *(Conceding this is a better idea)* Well, I heard a lot of

23   kids were kinda sick of Sierra's parties and weren't

24   going to go.

25   MEGAN: Perfect! Kelsey, you bring the soda!

26   QUINCHE: I'm bringing double chocolate chip ice cream!

44. Dating by Phone

Topic: Who isn't nervous making that first date phone call?

Cast:
TINA: the typical popular, self-confident girl
GREG: the typical unpopular, insecure guy

1   *(Scene takes place with TINA and GREG on opposite sides of*
2   *the stage, each on phones. No eye contact should be made.)*
3 **TINA: Hello?**
4 **GREG:** *(Voice wobbly)* **Hello?**
5 **TINA: Hello?**
6 **GREG: Oh, um,** *(Coughs)* **hi.**
7 **TINA: Who is this?**
8 **GREG: Oh, it's Greg.**
9 **TINA: Greg?**
10 **GREG: Yeah.**
11 **TINA:** *(Questioningly)* **Do I know you?**
12 **GREG: Oh, yeah, sure. We're in art class together.**
13 **TINA: Oh. Are you the tall guy with the red hair?**
14 **GREG: No, I'm the short guy with glasses.**
15 **TINA: Oh.**
16 **GREG: I sit behind Brent.**
17 **TINA:** *(Still obviously clueless)* **OK.**
18 **GREG: You still have no idea who I am, do you?**
19 **TINA: Sorry. I'm trying to remember.**
20 **GREG: I know. I have one of those forgettable faces. Not**
21   **you, though.**
22 **TINA: Huh?**
23 **GREG: Your face. It's remember-able. I mean memora-bilia.**
24   **I mean you're beautiful.**
25 **TINA:** *(Starting to frown into the phone)* **Oh. Uh, thanks, I**
26   **think.**

1 GREG: I'm sorry this is totally wrong.

2 TINA: What is?

3 GREG: The truth is I've been trying to get up the nerve for

4   like a month to talk to you at school.

5 TINA: *(Noncommittal)* Oh.

6 GREG: It's really hard for a guy like me to talk to a girl like

7   you.

8 TINA: What do you mean? What's a "girl like me"?

9 GREG: You know, smart, beautiful, popular. You always

10   have like two hundred people around you and a hundred

11   and ninety of them are boys.

12 TINA: That's not exactly true.

13 GREG: It's hard for a guy like me to approach someone like

14   you.

15 TINA: Well, what's a "guy like you"?

16 GREG: Not particularly smart, average looking, and only

17   popular with my dog.

18 TINA: I'm sure that's not true. Aren't you on student

19   council?

20 GREG: You *do* know who I am?

21 TINA: Yeah, I think so now.

22 GREG: *(Amazed)* Wow. You actually noticed me.

23 TINA: Well, aren't you that guy who stood up at the

24   assembly and asked Mrs. Krebs if she would let us have

25   a dress down day for Valentine's Day?

26 GREG: Yeah, that was me. Right.

27 TINA: Well, that was pretty brave.

28 GREG: *(Pleased)* You think?

29 TINA: Sure. It's hard to get up in front of everybody.

30   Especially Mrs. Krebs.

31 GREG: *(Becoming more comfortable)* Aw, she's not so bad.

32   She's nice.

33 TINA: *(Smiling)* I'm scared to death of her.

34 GREG: You shouldn't be. She's actually really nice. She

35   dropped a whole pile of papers in the hall once and I

1   stopped to help her. I've been golden ever since.
2 TINA: That's cool. I'll have to remember that next time I'm
3   tardy and get sent to her office. I'll bring you as a
4   bodyguard.
5 GREG: Love to. At your service. *(Pauses.)* Well, I guess you
6   wonder why I called.
7 TINA: Yeah, a little.
8 GREG: I was going to ask you if you have a date to the
9   Valentine's Day dance.
10 TINA: *(No expression)* Oh.
11 GREG: That doesn't sound like a good *oh.*
12 TINA: What's a "good oh"?
13 GREG: You know, like *(Pretending to swoon with joy)* Oh,
14   darling Greg, I'd just *die of joy* to go to the dance with
15   you.
16 TINA: *(Laughs.)* What kind of *oh* was it?
17 GREG: More like the *(Looking grossed out and bored)* how-in-
18   the-world-am-I-gonna-get-off-the-phone-with-this-loser
19   oh.
20 TINA: *(Laughs again.)* You're funny.
21 GREG: OK, what's the verdict? Oh A or Oh B?
22 TINA: Well, to be honest —
23 GREG: Here it comes.
24 TINA: No, give me a minute. I was gonna say it was neither.
25   You just caught me off guard.
26 GREG: You already have a date.
27 TINA: No, I don't.
28 GREG: *(Amazed)* You don't? You're kidding?
29 TINA: Is that so hard to believe?
30 GREG: *Yes!* I mean, a girl like you —
31 TINA: Yeah, yeah, whatever. All those "guys" you see
32   around me all the time are just friends and wouldn't ever
33   ask me to a dance.
34 GREG: Does that mean a normal guy like me has a chance?
35 TINA: I don't know if I'd call you normal, Greg.

128

1 GREG: *(Singing)* She remembers my name!

2 TINA: Calm down, crazy boy. And the answer is yes.

3 GREG: Yes?

4 TINA: Yes, I'll go to the dance with you.

5 GREG: You've got to be kidding!

6 TINA: Are you taking back your invitation?

7 GREG: *(Very excited)* No, no! This is terrific! This is

8   awesome! This is completely unexpected and I have no

9   idea what to say now.

10 TINA: How about saying "Bye. I'll see you in art class

11   tomorrow"?

12 GREG: *Yes!* Bye, Tina. I'll see you in art class tomorrow.

13 TINA: Good job. Bye. *(They hang up.)*

45. Look! Up in the Sky!

Topic: A kid pulls a prank on his clueless friends.

Cast:
CODY: the instigator and practical jokester
MARTA, PENNY, and LILY: innocent and clueless victims of Cody's

Note
All characters' constant staring upward during this skit necessitates that it be memorized as soon as possible.

1   *(CODY is staring up at the sky. MARTA enters.)*

2 MARTA: Hi.

3 CODY: *(Keeps staring up.)* **Hi.**

4 MARTA: *(Notices but doesn't comment.)* **How did you do on**

5   **that Spanish test today?**

6 CODY: Terrible.

7 MARTA: Yeah, me too. Señor Pedro never shows any mercy.

8   *(Pause. She looks up.)* **What are you looking at?**

9 CODY: I don't know.

10 MARTA: **What do you mean you don't know?** *(PENNY and*

11   *LILY enter.)*

12 PENNY: Hi, guys. What's up?

13 MARTA: *(She continues to stare up. Pauses.)* **I just don't know.**

14 PENNY: You don't know? *(She glances up.)*

15 LILY: What is everyone staring at? *(She looks up.)*

16 CODY: We don't know.

17 LILY: What does it look like?

18 PENNY: I think I see it.

19 MARTA: Where?

20 PENNY: *(Points.)* There.

21 LILY: I don't see it.

22 MARTA: I think I see it.

23 PENNY: What do you think it is?

1 LILY: Oh, my gosh, do you think it's a spaceship?

2 MARTA: It's probably just an airplane or something.

3 LILY: I still don't see it.

4 MARTA: It's right *there.*

5 LILY: *(Hesitantly)* Oh ... OK. Now I think I see it. *(CODY*

6 *carefully edges away from the GIRLS. He looks at them, puts*

7 *his hand over his mouth, and runs off laughing.)*

8 MARTA: It's not very big.

9 PENNY: That doesn't mean anything. It could still be a

10 spaceship.

11 LILY: Yeah. Maybe it's just really far away.

12 MARTA: I always wanted to see a UFO.

13 LILY: Do you think it will abduct us?

14 PENNY: If it did, we wouldn't remember. I read that

15 somewhere. *(Suddenly MARTA looks down and looks*

16 *around for CODY.)*

17 MARTA: Where's Cody? *(PENNY and LILY also look down and*

18 *around.)*

19 PENNY: He was just here!

20 LILY: Oh, no! He's been abducted! By aliens!

21 PENNY: Oh, no! I just knew it!

22 MARTA: We'd better go tell someone quick! *(They exit.)*

46. Missing Teacher

Topic: Exactly how long are you supposed to wait for a teacher before getting a free period?

Cast:

DEIDRE: bossy, impatient with the boys
KYLE: practical, would like a free period
JOEY: anxious to be free
ANASTASIA: cautious, trying to do the right thing
RYAN: worried about repercussions
JACOB: the class clown, easy going
JOHN: enjoys stirring up trouble

1   *(Scene should be set with students in desks arranged in*
2   *rows. GIRLS and RYAN should be reading or working in*
3   *workbooks. Others can be sleeping, doodling, throwing paper*
4   *airplanes, anything except working.)*
5   MIKE: How long are we supposed to wait?
6   DEIDRE: *(Reading, looks up from her book.)* **Just be quiet and**
7   **read or something.**
8   KYLE: Yeah, like that's gonna happen with *this* group.
9   JOEY: I think if she's not here in like five minutes we get a
10   free period.
11 ANASTASIA: You wish.
12 RYAN: You guys better be quiet. We're gonna get in trouble
13   when she comes in.
14 JACOB: *If* she comes.
15 JOHN: Maybe she's dead somewhere.
16 DEIDRE: *(Disdainful)* Don't be ridiculous.
17 MIKE: It could happen. People die all the time.
18 DEIDRE: Oh, good grief.
19 JACOB: No, really. Suppose she fell in the bathroom and hit
20   her head or something?
21 ANASTASIA: Jacob, you need a reality check. She'll be

1   here. She just got tied up on the phone or something.
2   JOEY: I *know* it says something in the handbook about if a
3   teacher isn't in the room by a certain time —
4   RYAN: What? You get to go crazy and hang from the lights?
5   MIKE: Sounds good to me.
6   JACOB: Sounds like regular class to me.
7   DEIDRE: I'm telling you guys to sit down and be quiet or
8   we're all gonna get punished.
9   JOEY: Does anyone have any food?
10 ANASTASIA: If you get food out, you're *really* gonna get in
11   trouble.
12 MIKE: *(Shifts position and whines.)* I'm bored.
13 KYLE: You're always bored.
14 RYAN: I think we should just go ahead and read the next
15   chapter while we're waiting.
16 MIKE: You know, Ryan, you sure know how to ruin a good
17   time.
18 JOEY: Yeah, we can at least *pretend* she's not coming and
19   we're gonna have a free period.
20 DEIDRE: And you could *read* and actually use your time for
21   something productive.
22 JACOB: Hey, I have an idea. Why don't *you* read while we
23   play Hangman on the board? Then you can tell us what
24   happened and we won't have to read it.
25 DEIDRE: Wouldn't that be kind of cheating?
26 MIKE: No, I think it's called cooperative learning. Working
27   together, you know.
28 ANASTASIA: Except we do all the work.
29 JOEY: Exactly.
30 KYLE: I'm bored.
31 RYAN: I think one of us should go to Mrs. Taylor's office and
32   tell her.
33 JACOB, JOE, and MIKE: *(Shouting)* No!
34 JACOB: What, are you crazy?
35 MIKE: Yeah, why would you do that?

1 ANASTASIA: I just know we're gonna get in trouble.

2 RYAN: Listen! I think I hear her coming!

3 JOEY: Dang it! Another fun episode ruined.

4 MIKE: We're gonna get in trouble anyway for not doing

5   anything.

6 DEIDRE: I did something. I *read.*

7 JACOB: No you didn't. You just yelled at us the whole time.

8 KYLE: Back into position, men! At least pretend you're

9   being good until she figures it out.

10 ANASTASIA: *(Sarcastically)* Yeah. Good idea. That should

11   work.

47. Unlikely Allies

Topic: Two family pets, a cat and a dog, work through their differences for a common goal.

Cast:
FLUFFY: arrogant, superior, disdainful of Spot
SPOT: fun-loving, cautious, not thrilled with Fluffy

1   *(Scene opens with ANIMALS meeting Center Stage. No*
2   *costumes are necessary but can be used.)*
3 FLUFFY: *(Not nice)* **What are *you* doing here?**
4 SPOT: **I could ask you the same question.**
5 FLUFFY: *(Sarcastically)* **I'm nocturnal, goofball.**
6 SPOT: **Oh, right. I forgot.**
7 FLUFFY: **Shocking.**
8 SPOT: *(Distracted)* **Didn't you hear that noise?**
9 FLUFFY: **You mean your snoring?**
10 SPOT: **No, it was a crunching sound. Sounded like someone**
11   **might be outside walking around the house.**
12 FLUFFY: *(Dismissively)* **Nonsense.**
13 SPOT: **Look, we dogs know a thing or two about keeping**
14   **watch.**
15 FLUFFY: **Spare me the self-promoting publicity campaign.**
16 SPOT: **It wouldn't hurt you to be a little more protective,**
17   **you know.**
18 FLUFFY: *(Snotty)* **You've got to be kidding.**
19 SPOT: **Don't you want to take care of Bryan and Monica?**
20 FLUFFY: **Heavens no. Why should I care about them?**
21 SPOT: **Because they take care of you, give you a place to**
22   **live, and feed you.**
23 FLUFFY: **Oh joy.**
24 SPOT: **You're really very ungrateful, you know.**
25 FLUFFY: **I couldn't care less about the humans who live**
26   **with me.**

1   SPOT: What would you do if something happened to them,
2   huh? Then what would you do?
3   FLUFFY: Continue on my life as if nothing happened. I can't
4   imagine there being any change.
5   SPOT: That shows what *you* know. If Bryan and Monica
6   weren't here, someone would take us to the pound.
7   FLUFFY: What in the world is that?
8   SPOT: It's a prisoner of war camp for animals.
9   FLUFFY: *(Refusing to believe)* You're crazy.
10 SPOT: No, I'm serious! They put you in cages and stick you
11   with needles. People come in to look at you and stick
12   their fingers in your cage and touch you and yell in your
13   face.
14 FLUFFY: Nonsense.
15 SPOT: But the worst part is what happens after a few days
16   and no person decides you'd make a good, sweet pet,
17   which in your case is a sure bet.
18 FLUFFY: What could possibly happen?
19 SPOT: They kill you.
20 FLUFFY: They do not.
21 SPOT: Yes, they do. I swear.
22 FLUFFY: Spot, you are the dumbest animal ever born. How
23   in the world would you know something like that?
24 SPOT: Ranger next door told me. He was there for a couple
25   of days before the Griffins decided to bring him home. He
26   said they lost a lot of good men out there.
27 FLUFFY: You believe a two-year-old Jack Russell who
28   chases his tail all day long?
29 SPOT: Yes! I know it's true. What else do you think happens
30   when pets have no homes? You think they go live in the
31   wild and scrounge for food to survive?
32 FLUFFY: *(Long pause)* I never thought about it. I've always
33   had a nice home, and so has everyone I know.
34 SPOT: Well, it doesn't go down that way. Face it, we
35   animals are dependent upon humans to treat us well, or

1   else we'd starve and die.

2   FLUFFY: I actually like Monica. She is very sweet to me and

3   slips me those fish shaped crackers when Bryan isn't

4   looking.

5   SPOT: That's what I mean. We have it made here and we

6   should do everything we can to keep it that way.

7   FLUFFY: *(Conceding)* So what's your plan?

8   SPOT: I try to patrol the house. I keep my ears open for

9   strange sounds, or to make sure Bryan and Monica are

10   OK while they're here. I just have trouble keeping awake

11   at night and that's when trouble usually happens.

12 FLUFFY: Well, I'm always up all night. This might be

13   something to keep me from going absolutely crazy from

14   boredom. What would I have to do?

15 SPOT: Just watch, look, and listen. Anything unusual, you

16   come get me.

17 FLUFFY: I come get you?

18 SPOT: Right.

19 FLUFFY: So I do nothing but come get you.

20 SPOT: Well, let's face it, you're not exactly ... intimidating.

21 FLUFFY: And you are?

22 SPOT: I can at least bark and let the family know

23   something's up.

24 FLUFFY: You've got a point. My hiss isn't very loud.

25 SPOT: And you have excellent vision so you can see in the

26   dark.

27 FLUFFY: *(Preening)* I do indeed.

28 SPOT: I think between the two of us we should be able to

29   guard this place fairly well.

30 FLUFFY: I really wasn't looking for a career at this point in

31   my life.

32 SPOT: It won't be much work. Honest. Just keep your ears

33   open.

34 FLUFFY: My ears are *always* open.

35 SPOT: Good. And remember, what do you do when you see

1   something suspicious?

2   FLUFFY: *(Sighs.)* I come get you.

3   SPOT: Right. I think we're ready. I'm gonna go grab some

4   shut-eye and you can take the first shift.

5   FLUFFY: Aye aye, Captain. *(SPOT exits. FLUFFY settles down*

6   *for a nap.)* Man's best friend. Huh.

48. Your Space

Topic: Friends discuss the problems with networking Websites.

Cast:
CAMREN: funny, naïve, having trouble understanding all the fuss
DONNIE and JOSH: concerned friends
COLLEEN: wiser and in the know

1   *(Scene opens with ALL sitting or standing Center Stage.)*

2   **CAMREN:** *(Obviously concerned)* **I am in so much trouble.**

3   **DONNIE: Why? What's up?**

4   **CAMREN: My mom saw my MySpace yesterday.**

5   **JOSH:** *(Understands.)* **Oh no.**

6   **CAMREN: Yeah, she flipped.**

7   **COLLEEN: What's wrong with your mom seeing your**
8   **MySpace?**

9   **JOSH: You obviously haven't seen Carmen's MySpace.**

10 **COLLEEN: No, I guess I haven't.**

11 **DONNIE: You would understand if you had.**

12 **CAMREN: It's not that bad.**

13 **DONNIE: Sure it is.**

14 **JOSH: It's the worst one ever.**

15 **COLLEEN: What's wrong with it?**

16 **CAMREN: Nothing. It's cool.**

17 **JOSH: No, it's not. You've got the weirdest stuff on there.**

18 **DONNIE: Yeah. I won't even go on your page because it's so**
19   **weird.**

20 **CAMREN: You guys are wussies.**

21 **COLLEEN: What kind of weird stuff?**

22 **CAMREN: Nothing! It's perfectly fine.**

23 **DONNIE: Under** *hobbies* **he has "drinking and drugs."**

24 **COLLEEN:** *(Shocked)* **What?**

25 **CAMREN: It was a joke!**

1 JOSH: And under *favorite people* he has Hitler and Jeffrey
2   Dahmer.
3 COLLEEN: Carmen!
4 CAMREN: Gosh, it's just a joke. Nobody puts real stuff on
5   their MySpace.
6 COLLEEN: I do.
7 CAMREN: Nobody but you.
8 DONNIE: I know people exaggerate and put goofy stuff on
9   there, but not like yours.
10 JOSH: Yeah. Yours is just weird.
11 CAMREN: Nobody has a sense of humor anymore. My
12   mom's all worried about high schools seeing it and not
13   letting me in.
14 COLLEEN: I heard that happened. My sister went to school
15   with a girl who had Satan worshipping stuff on her
16   MySpace and Barksdale Academy didn't take her
17   because of it.
18 CAMREN: That's not fair. It's none of their business. It's
19   private.
20 JOSH: No, it's not. It's public information. That's the whole
21   point.
22 CAMREN: Maybe so, but what business does a school have
23   looking at it? It's just for fun. And it's supposed to be
24   for kids. Old people don't understand.
25 COLLEEN: *I* don't understand. Why would you want to put
26   all that goofy stuff on a site and pretend it's you? It's like
27   those kids with the twelve inch Mohawks who complain
28   because everyone is always staring at them.
29 DONNIE: Yeah. You look like you're either a really awful kid
30   or you're just dying for that kind of attention. Either
31   way, it gives people a bad impression of you.
32 CAMREN: My profile is private. No one can find it if I don't
33   let them.
34 JOSH: *(Wisely)* Oh, naïve one, people have their ways.
35 DONNIE: Schools hire people just to do that kind of thing.

1   You don't have to be a P.I. to be able to find stuff on the
2   Internet. Anybody can do it. And they make a living
3   doing it.

4 CAMREN: Are you guys telling me I have to take out the
5   murder rap song?

6 COLLEEN: Yes.

7 CAMREN: And the gory pictures?

8 JOSH: Yes. And the profanity. And the *school you go to* and
9   *sports* you play. What, are you some type of idiot?

10 CAMREN: What?

11 JOSH: Strangers can totally find you, you know. You put a
12   lot of personal stuff on there.

13 CAMREN: That's not true.

14 DONNIE: Yes, it is. You said you go to Hampton Middle, play
15   basketball, and wear number eighty-three. Duh. Anyone
16   in the world could find you. *(Silence)*

17 CAMREN: *(Beginning to understand)* I never thought of it that
18   way.

19 JOSH: Doesn't look like you're doing much thinking at all
20   these days.

21 COLLEEN: Besides not wanting you to look stupid, Carmen,
22   we want you to be safe. There are a lot of crazy people
23   out there.

24 CAMREN: There are a lot of crazy people in here.

25 DONNIE: Maybe. But at least you know our craziness. Who
26   knows what's creeping through the Internet looking for a
27   cute little boy just like you?

28 CAMREN: Cut it out.

29 COLLEEN: Look, I'll help you design something really cool.
30   There are some awesome sites where you can download
31   really cool graphics and you can put up *normal* music
32   from your favorite bands.

33 JOSH: And then maybe I'll consider being your friend.

34 CAMREN: If I let you.

35 JOSH: You'll let me. After the way your site looks now,

1   you'll be lucky to have *anyone* want to be your friend!
2 CAMREN: You guys are saints.
3 DONNIE: That's what I keep telling you.

49. Babysitters

Topic: Two girls discuss different perspectives of working as a teen.

Cast:
RYCE: disillusioned, not thrilled about the prospect of baby-sitting
CLEO: more appreciative of the rare opportunity to make good money

1   *(Scene opens with GIRLS chatting Center Stage.)*
2   RYCE: *(Glumly)* I'm so bummed about tonight.
3   CLEO: What's wrong?
4   RYCE: I have to baby-sit.
5   CLEO: Ugh. The kiss of death. Who?
6   RYCE: Two brats down the street.
7   CLEO: How old?
8   RYCE: Seven and four.
9   CLEO: Sounds like lots of fun.
10 RYCE: The seven-year-old is OK, but the four-year-old is
11   whiny and cries for his mom the whole time.
12 CLEO: Do they let you use the phone?
13 RYCE: Yeah, but only after the kids are in bed. Which is
14   never. Kevin cries and cries and I try everything but he
15   usually falls asleep like five minutes before his parents
16   come home.
17 CLEO: Is it good money?
18 RYCE: Yeah. I get twelve dollars an hour.
19 CLEO: *(Can't believe it.)* What? You're kidding.
20 RYCE: No. Why?
21 CLEO: That's a ton of money. How many hours?
22 RYCE: Usually no more than four. I'll probably get fifty
23   dollars tonight.
24 CLEO: *(Emphatically)* You've *got* to be kidding. Fifty dollars
25   for watching two kids? And no diapers?
26 RYCE: No, no diapers. But Kevin is a real brat, I'm telling
27   you.

1 CLEO: *(Wistfully)* I wish I had a job like that.

2 RYCE: No, you don't. I'm telling you, it's no fun.

3 CLEO: Since when is work supposed to be fun?

4 RYCE: Well, I would rather go shopping or to the movies or

5 something.

6 CLEO: I'll tell you what, I'll take your baby-sitting job and

7 *make* money and you go shopping and *spend* money.

8 How's that?

9 RYCE: No way! I like the money.

10 CLEO: So you're saying the job isn't all that bad after all?

11 RYCE: I hate it but I love the money.

12 CLEO: Ryce, we are looking at the future as adults. Like my

13 dad always says, you don't have to love your work, but

14 you do have to work.

15 RYCE: *(Sarcastically)* That sounds exactly like the future I

16 want.

17 CLEO: Well, you don't intend to baby-sit the rest of your life,

18 do you? Where else can a thirteen-year-old make that

19 kind of money?

20 RYCE: *(Sighs.)* You're right. Nowhere.

21 CLEO: Right. I'm lucky if I get ten dollars for cleaning out

22 the shed. I have to ask my mom for every penny I get to

23 spend.

24 RYCE: True. It is really nice having my own money.

25 CLEO: And fifty dollars! That's a *ton* of money!

26 RYCE: Yeah, you're right.

27 CLEO: No more complaining about the gravy boat you're

28 riding, OK?

29 RYCE: OK, fine. I won't complain.

30 CLEO: Sure you don't want to trade?

31 RYCE: No way. Now that you've made me understand how

32 good a job this is there's no way I'm giving it away!

33 CLEO: Figures. I just talked myself out of fifty dollars.

34 RYCE: Yeah. Thanks. *(She smiles.)*

50. Going Out

Topic: Four friends try to find something to do on their night together.

Cast:
SHEILA, BETSY, MARY, and JONI: the typical, easygoing kids

1   *(Scene opens with BETSY, MARY, and JONI standing Center*
2   *Stage, jackets and purses in hand. SHEILA enters while*
3   *putting on a jacket and joins them.)*
4   SHEILA: I'm ready! Where are we going?
5   BETSY: *(Shrugs.)* I don't care.
6   MARY: Where do you all want to go?
7   JONI: Anywhere.
8   MARY: Anywhere like where?
9   SHEILA: We could go to the movies.
10 MARY: *(Only slightly curious)* What's playing?
11 JONI: That new Derek Price movie is out.
12 SHEILA: *(Disdainfully)* He's a dork.
13 JONI: He is not. He's nice.
14 MARY: *(With passion)* I hate Derek Price. He's such a phony.
15 BETSY: *(Whining)* I don't want to go to the movies.
16 JONI: Well, what do you want to do?
17 BETSY: *(Bored)* I don't know.
18 SHEILA: We could go bowling.
19 JONI: *(Emphatically)* I hate to bowl.
20 MARY: Me too. I stink at it.
21 BETSY: *(Whining)* I don't want to bowl.
22 JONI: So what should we do? *(ALL pause.)*
23 SHEILA: We could go to Griffin's for a burger or something.
24 MARY: I just finished dinner.
25 JONI: Me too. *(ALL pause.)*
26 BETSY: This is pathetic, you know.
27 MARY: Yeah, we finally get a night we're all free and we

1   can't think of what to do.
2 SHEILA: There's a football game tonight at school.
3 MARY: I hope Richie Thompson breaks his leg.
4 BETSY: That's not nice.
5 MARY: He's a jerk. He never does his homework and then
6   wants to copy mine.
7 JONI: What's that got to do with the football game?
8 MARY: He's the star of the team!
9 BETSY: *(To SHEILA)* Do you want to go to the game?
10 SHEILA: No.
11 BETSY: Then why did you suggest it?
12 SHEILA: I didn't. I just mentioned there was a game. *(ALL*
13   *pause.)*
14 MARY: Sorenson's has a new ice cream flavor.
15 JONI: What is it?
16 MARY: Banana chocolate brownie chip.
17 SHEILA: *(Makes a face.)* Gross.
18 BETSY: Yum!
19 JONI: I think that sounds good!
20 SHEILA: I'm gonna puke.
21 MARY: It's good! I had some last week.
22 JONI: Let's go there.
23 BETSY: Yeah, that's something to do at least. Maybe some
24   of the kids are hanging out there.
25 SHEILA: If anyone orders that banana chocolate ice cream,
26   I'm gonna puke on them.
27 MARY: Is there anything that *doesn't* make you puke?
28 SHEILA: *(Looking at MARY)* Nothing I can think of at the
29   moment.

51. Give Me a Break

Topic: Friends develop a case of cast-envy when a friend breaks his arm.

Cast:
JONAH: has arm in a cast, looks at the bright side
DAMIAN: a lady-killer
CLYVE: a jokester

1 *(Scene opens with DAMIAN and CLYVE watching JONAH*
2 *enter and join them.)*
3 DAMIAN: Dang, Jonah, what happened?
4 JONAH: Man, I broke my arm skateboarding.
5 CLYVE: I knew you were gonna do that. How many times
6   have I told you that you're never gonna land an ollie?
7 JONAH: *(Sarcastically)* Thanks, Clyve, that makes me feel
8   much better.
9 DAMIAN: Does it hurt?
10 JONAH: *(Runs his opposite hand up and down the cast.)* Not
11   too much right now. It did when I did it.
12 CLYVE: How long you got to wear the cast?
13 JONAH: *(Disgustedly)* Four to six weeks.
14 DAMIAN: *(Appalled)* No way!
15 CLYVE: There goes swim team.
16 JONAH: Yeah, no kidding.
17 DAMIAN: I hate swim team.
18 CLYVE: Me too.
19 JONAH: Me too. *(Pauses.)* Hey, why do we all go if we hate
20   it?
21 CLYVE: *(Wondering)* I have no idea. I thought you liked it.
22 JONAH: No way.
23 DAMIAN: So you get out of swim team now for the summer?
24 JONAH: Yeah. And the way I figure it, I'll just phase out and
25   won't have to do it next summer either.

1   CLYVE: *(Inspired)* **Dude, that's awesome.**

2   DAMIAN: *(Wistfully)* **I wish I had a broken arm.**

3   CLYVE: **Hold out your arm, Damian!**

4   DAMIAN: **Oh, ha ha.**

5   JONAH: **Look at this, guys.** *(They look closely at his cast.)*

6   CLYVE: **Does that say Pamela Houston?**

7   JONAH: *(Proudly)* **Indeed it does.**

8   DAMIAN: *(Very impressed)* **No way. Pamela Houston signed**
9   **your cast?**

10 JONAH: **She did.**

11 CLYVE: *(Also impressed)* **Dude, how did you manage that?**

12 JONAH: *(With animation)* **She saw me in the hallway and got**
13   **all sympathetic and asked if she could sign it. I acted all**
14   **cool and said, "Sure, if you want." She pulled out a**
15   **Sharpie and then wrote her name. And, look, she even**
16   **put a little heart.** *(They ALL lean in to get a closer look.)*

17 CLYVE: **You are *soooo* lucky!**

18 DAMIAN: **How did she smell? I've never gotten that close to**
19   **her.**

20 CLYVE: **Man, you are just weird.**

21 JONAH: **She smelled *great*.**

22 DAMIAN: *(Emphatically)* **I knew it.**

23 CLYVE: **So you're saying the hottest girl in school just**
24   **walked up to you, started a conversation with you, and**
25   **offered to sign your cast? Man, I didn't even know she**
26   **knew your name.**

27 JONAH: **I know! Me neither! It's like a chick magnet, I'm**
28   **telling you. I walk down the hall or go to the store and**
29   **they all look at my arm and smile and shake their heads**
30   **a little like, "poor baby, he's got a boo-boo."**

31 DAMIAN: *(Very jealous)* **You stink, you know that?**

32 JONAH: *(Confused)* **Why, because I broke my arm?**

33 DAMIAN: **No, because you found the only way I haven't tried**
34   **to attract female attention.**

35 JONAH: **Well, I didn't plan it, let me tell you.**

1 CLYVE: *And* you get out of swim team.

2 JONAH: Bonus.

3 CLYVE: Shoot. Sign me up.

4 DAMIAN: Yeah, I think I'll crank up my skateboarding

5   practices.

6 CLYVE: With your luck, you'll break your nose or something

7   and then you'll be even uglier than you are.

8 DAMIAN: You're just the funniest guy around, aren't you?

9 CLYVE: Hey, Jonah, let me buy you a soda. Do you think

10   you could toss some of those extra babes my way?

11 JONAH: Don't see why not. Spread the wealth, that's my

12   motto.

13 DAMIAN: Now he's a regular matchmaker.

14 CLYVE: Hey, I'll take whatever I can get.

52. A Tangled Web

Topic: Two girls discuss the downside of lying.

Cast:
MARCIE: easily picks up on liars and calls them on it
MARY: struggling to get herself out of her deception

1   *(Scene opens with MARCIE joining MARY On-Stage.)*
2   **MARCIE: Hi, Mary.**
3   **MARY:** *(Overly cheerful)* **Oh, hi, Marcie. How are you?**
4   **MARCIE: Fine, fine. Um, what did you say you had to do last**
5   **Sunday so that you couldn't come to my recital?**
6   **MARY:** *(Immediately uncomfortable)* **Oh, it was my cousin's**
7   **birthday. The party was out of town.**
8   **MARCIE: Mmmmhmmmm. How old is your cousin?**
9   **MARY:** *(Pauses to think.)* **Eight. I think.**
10   **MARCIE: Right.** *(Slight pause and then she decides to speak her*
11   *mind)* **You know, Mary, I don't appreciate your lying to**
12   **me.**
13   **MARY:** *(Falsely innocent)* **I'm not lying!**
14   **MARCIE: I know you didn't go to some birthday party on**
15   **Sunday. In fact, I know just where you were.**
16   **MARY:** *(Still maintaining her innocence)* **That's not true. I did**
17   **too go to the party!**
18   **MARCIE: You were at the mall with Tiffany Jacobs.**
19   **MARY:** *(Emphatically)* **I was not!**
20   **MARCIE: Mary, my brother was standing behind you in line**
21   **at the yogurt place.**
22   **MARY:** *(Starting to get trapped)* **I was not at the mall. He must**
23   **be mistaken.**
24   **MARCIE: You two were talking about Jason.**
25   **MARY:** *(Much less confident in her ability to pull this off)* **That**
26   **wasn't me.**

1 MARCIE: It *was.* *(Angry, but more hurt than anything)* I hate
2   being lied to.
3 MARY: *(Still trying but losing steam)* It must have been
4   somebody that looked like me. I swear I wasn't at the
5   mall.
6 MARCIE: If you didn't want to come to my recital, you could
7   have just told me.
8 MARY: *(One last-ditch effort)* I'm telling you, your brother is
9   wrong.
10 MARCIE: I asked Tiffany.
11 MARY: *(Pauses.)* Yeah?
12 MARCIE: Why would you lie to me?
13 MARY: *(Pauses. Then suddenly has an idea)* Oh, he must have
14   seen me at night, long after your recital. We did go the
15   mall then, but that was after I got home from the party.
16 MARCIE: It was twelve thirty. He had to work at one so he
17   knows what time it was.
18 MARY: *(Trying to turn the tables)* What, is your brother like
19   your spy now?
20 MARCIE: Don't change the subject. Why didn't you tell me
21   the truth?
22 MARY: *(Sighs. Surrenders.)* I didn't want to hurt your feelings.
23 MARCIE: Well, they're hurt now.
24 MARY: *(Sincere but embarrassed)* I'm sorry.
25 MARCIE: You know, lying never accomplishes anything.
26 MARY: *(Disgruntled)* I know.
27 MARCIE: No, you don't. You lie all the time.
28 MARY: *(Affronted)* I do not!
29 MARCIE: You forget I was with you when you told your mom
30   on the phone that we were doing homework when we
31   were watching *Lost.*
32 MARY: *(Defensive)* She would have yelled at me.
33 MARCIE: And when you told Peter Becker you were going to
34   your grandmother's when you were really going out with
35   John Kramer.

1   MARY: John is way cuter.

2   MARCIE: And when you told Mrs. Winters you were up all

3   night with your sick dog and couldn't do your homework.

4   MARY: I could have a dog.

5   MARCIE: My point is, Mary, that you lie a lot and people

6   know it. Now no one trusts you.

7   MARY: *(Suspiciously)* What are you talking about?

8   MARCIE: Everyone knows you lie all the time. We only

9   believe about half of what comes out of your mouth. It

10   doesn't make for a very good friendship.

11 MARY: *(Getting offended)* That's not very nice.

12 MARCIE: *(Also hurt)* Well, lying isn't very nice either. It's like

13   saying you don't trust us.

14 MARY: What are you talking about?

15 MARCIE: If you had told me the truth, that you just didn't

16   want to come to the recital, but thanks for asking, that

17   would have been better than lying about it.

18 MARY: You would have been upset with me.

19 MARCIE: *(Trying to explain)* A little, but less upset than I am

20   now, knowing you lied. You should have just told Peter

21   that he was nice but no thanks, you didn't want to go

22   out with him.

23 MARY: *(Also trying to be understood)* That would have been

24   really hard. And it would have hurt his feelings.

25 MARCIE: You sound like you're worried about everyone's

26   feelings, but I think you just don't want to deal with

27   people giving you a hard time about what you do.

28 MARY: Well, who likes to be given a hard time? I'd rather

29   just put it off and the person may never know.

30 MARCIE: *(Reasonably)* Yeah, but how long did Peter chase

31   you and keep asking you out until Candice — not you, by

32   the way — told him you just weren't interested?

33 MARY: *(Quietly)* It was a few weeks.

34 MARCIE: Try months. That was just cruel. If you'd been

35   honest but nice, he would have been upset but at least

1   he would have moved on sooner.

2 MARY: I guess.

3 MARCIE: My mom says you never really *have* to lie. It just
4   takes some creativity.

5 MARY: *(Sarcastically)* Yeah, sure.

6 MARCIE: OK, say we're shopping and I try on a pair of pants
7   and they make my butt look huge. I know they do but
8   they're cute, so I ask you if they make my butt look big.
9   What do you say?

10 MARY: I say, "No, of course not."

11 MARCIE: Right. That *is* what you'd say. That's a lie.

12 MARY: What am I supposed to say? "Yes, Marcie, you look
13   like a cow."

14 MARCIE: No, but how about, "I liked the other pair better,"
15   or "I don't like them."

16 MARY: Then you'll know I think your butt looks huge.

17 MARCIE: But I already know it! Don't you get it? I wouldn't
18   ask if I didn't already know it.

19 MARY: Then why did you ask?

20 MARCIE: It's just what people do. But you really don't have
21   to lie. You just have to be creative.

22 MARY: This sounds exhausting.

23 MARCIE: Can't be as exhausting as trying to keep up with
24   the wild stories you invent.

25 MARY: Yeah, sometimes that does get a little sticky.

26 MARCIE: So, you wanna come over and watch the videotape
27   of my recital?

28 MARY: *(Pause.)* Not really.

29 MARCIE: *(Laughs.)* Very good. That was a test.

30 MARY: Phew. I thought you might go ballistic on me.

31 MARCIE: Yeah, I'll get to that. What do you have against
32   violin recitals?

33 MARY: Oh, I think I have to go wash my hair ...

53. Chow Time

Topic: Three buddies discuss their different taste buds.

Cast:
NELSON: rather traditional in snacking patterns
EDDIE: a constant snacker, his taste is a little odd
DOM: sarcastic and funny

1   *(Scene starts with the BOYS sitting around playing video*
2   *games or watching TV.)*
3   **NELSON: You guys hungry?**
4   **EDDIE: Always.**
5   **DOM:** *(Enthusiastically)* **Yes! Got anything to eat?**
6   **NELSON:** *(Shaking head)* **You kidding? My mom hasn't been**
7   **to the store in like two years.**
8   **EDDIE: I'm starving. I haven't eaten in —**
9   **DOM:** *(Interrupts.)* **Minutes! You told me you had twelve**
10   **pancakes right before you came over.**
11   **EDDIE: Dude, that was breakfast. It's lunch time now.**
12   **NELSON: It's ten thirty.**
13   **EDDIE: Like I said, it's lunch time.**
14   **DOM:** *(Nonchalant)* **I could eat.**
15   **NELSON: You can always eat.**
16   **DOM: Unlike some people, I didn't have breakfast.**
17   **NELSON: We've got cereal.**
18   **EDDIE:** *(Makes buzzer sound.)* **Wrong answer, Nelson.**
19   **DOM: Yeah, cereal's lame.**
20   **NELSON: I eat cereal all the time. It's the one thing I know**
21   **we'll have in the house. Assuming we have milk, of**
22   **course.**
23   **EDDIE: What do you need milk for?**
24   **NELSON: To put on the cereal, fool.**
25   **EDDIE:** *(Grossed out)* **Ewwww! You put milk on cereal?**
26   **DOM: Ignore him, Nelson. He's got some bizarre eating**

154

1   habits. Trust me, you don't wanna know.

2 EDDIE: They're not weird. You're weird.

3 NELSON: Like what?

4 DOM: He puts mayonnaise on French fries.

5 NELSON: Ewwww!

6 EDDIE: It's good!

7 DOM: It's disgusting.

8 EDDIE: Have you ever tried it?

9 NELSON: I've never tried frogs' legs either, but I don't need

10   to eat them to know they're gross.

11 DOM: Yeah.

12 EDDIE: Frogs' legs are good!

13 NELSON: *(Aghast)* You're kidding, right?

14 DOM: I told you that you didn't want to know.

15 EDDIE: You guys live a sad and sheltered life. You've got to

16   live it up a little!

17 DOM: Eating frogs' legs and mayonnaise on French fries is

18   living it up?

19 EDDIE: Well, it's better than the steady diet of burgers and

20   pizza that you live on.

21 NELSON: Pizza is the complete food.

22 DOM: Yeah, you got your vegetables, the tomatoes. Protein,

23   the cheese. And bread, the crust.

24 EDDIE: Yeah, and extra protein with the salmon.

25 NELSON: *(Unbelieving)* Oh, no, don't say it.

26 EDDIE: *(Clueless)* Say what?

27 DOM: Yes, his mom puts baked salmon on their pizza.

28 EDDIE: *(Very innocent)* What's wrong with that? It goes really

29   well with the olives and pineapple.

30 NELSON: I'm suddenly not hungry any more.

31 EDDIE: Man, you've made me hungry for pizza now. Can we

32   order in?

33 DOM: If you get a pizza with salmon, pineapple, and olives

34   you *cannot* eat in the same room as us.

35 EDDIE: Why? You guys are wimps.

1   NELSON: I think you're seriously disturbed, Eddie.

2   EDDIE: Why? Because I have a varied, extensive, eclectic
3   palate?

4   DOM: What the heck does that mean?

5   NELSON: It means he eats weird stuff.

6   EDDIE: Exotic stuff, not weird. You guys are boring.

7   NELSON: Better boring than bizarre.

8   EDDIE: Huh! That's where you got it wrong! Bizarre is the
9   way to go.

10 DOM: You would know.

11 NELSON: Maybe sometimes, but not with pizza. Man, you
12   gotta keep the pizza simple. It's an American tradition.

13 EDDIE: Pizza is Italian.

14 NELSON: Whatever! You can't put fish on pizza. I think
15   that's against the law in like thirty-two states.

16 EDDIE: OK, Nelson, we'll get a pepperoni pizza and I'll suffer
17   through for your sake, because you're such a good
18   friend.

19 NELSON: You're a prince, Eddie.

20 DOM: You got any carry-out menus around?

21 NELSON: *(Looking around)* Yeah, somewhere.

22 EDDIE: Hey, while you're looking, see if you can find a sushi
23   menu.

24 DOM: I'm gonna punch you.

54. Just Going "Out"

Topic: A mom and daughter discuss the daughter's vague "going out" explanation.

Cast:
MEREDITH: deliberately trying to avoid the twenty questions from her mom
MOM: just trying to do her job

1   *(Scene opens with MOM sitting in a chair reading the paper.*
2   *MEREDITH tries to breeze by but gets stopped in her tracks.)*
3   **MEREDITH: Bye, Mom.**
4   **MOM:** *(Curious)* **Where are you going?**
5   **MEREDITH: Out.**
6   **MOM: Out where?**
7   **MEREDITH:** *(Trying to keep moving)* **Nowhere, just out.**
8   **MOM: Out is an adjective, Meredith, not a noun.**
9   **MEREDITH: Huh?**
10 **MOM:** *(Turns her full attention on MEREDITH.)* **Where are you**
11   **going? Specifically?**
12 **MEREDITH:** *(A little defensively)* **I don't know exactly yet.**
13 **MOM: What is that supposed to mean?**
14 **MEREDITH:** *(A little exasperated)* **It means I haven't decided**
15   **where I'm going yet.**
16 **MOM:** *(A little flip)* **Well, shouldn't you decide before you walk**
17   **out the door? Otherwise you'll just start walking and it**
18   **could be the wrong direction.**
19 **MEREDITH:** *(Whining)* **Moooom ...**
20 **MOM:** *(Stands and crosses to her.)* **I need to know where**
21   **you're going, Meredith.**
22 **MEREDITH:** *(Getting a little angry)* **Why? Don't you trust me?**
23 **MOM: Hmmmm. That's a very loaded question.**
24 **MEREDITH:** *(Offended)* **You *don't* trust me.**

1   MOM: *(Matter-of-factly)* I'm your mother. I get to ask where
2   you're going.
3   MEREDITH: I'm just going out with the girls. Nowhere
4   special.
5   MOM: Which "girls" are you going out with?
6   MEREDITH: Sammy, Alice, Cassie, Margie, and Jake.
7   MOM: Jake?
8   MEREDITH: Yeah.
9   MOM: Jake is one of the girls?
10   MEREDITH: *(Disdainful)* No, of course not.
11   MOM: Then why did you say you were going out with the
12   girls?
13   MEREDITH: *(Getting very bored)* Is there a point to all this?
14   MOM: *(Very serious)* Yes. The point is I want to know where
15   you're going and who you're going with.
16   MEREDITH: *(Emphatically)* Why?
17   MOM: It's in the mommy handbook. I'm supposed to know
18   where my thirteen-year-old daughter is at all times.
19   MEREDITH: Alice's mother never asks her where she's
20   going.
21   MOM: You don't really want to compare my mothering
22   techniques with Alice's mom's, do you?
23   MEREDITH: I'm just saying —
24   MOM: *(Cuts her off.)* Alice's mom might not care where she
25   is, but I care where you are.
26   MEREDITH: We're just gonna hang out at the mall.
27   MOM: Oh, OK. In that case, no.
28   MEREDITH: No what?
29   MOM: No, you can't go.
30   MEREDITH: *(Shocked)* Mom!
31   MOM: You're not going to "hang out at the mall."
32   MEREDITH: Why?
33   MOM: It's just not a good idea.
34   MEREDITH: *(Whiney and pleading)* C'mon, Mom, why not?
35   We're not doing anything.

1 MOM: Exactly. And since none of you have any money, it's
2   called *loitering* and the mall doesn't like it.
3 MEREDITH: We just walk around and look at stuff and talk.
4   We're not going to get into any trouble.
5 MOM: Why don't you hang out here?
6 MEREDITH: *(Appalled)* Here?
7 MOM: Yes, here. Where you live. Your house. Remember?
8 MEREDITH: That's boring, Mom. No one wants to just hang
9   out at home.
10 MOM: How about if I let you get fast food and play video
11   games?
12 MEREDITH: And Timmy will be driving us nuts all night.
13   He's a pain when I have people over.
14 MOM: I'll tell you what, I'll take Timmy out while you and
15   your friends hang out. I won't bring him home until it's
16   his bedtime and I promise I won't let him bug you.
17 MEREDITH: *(Suspicious)* Really? You'll let me and my friends
18   stay here alone?
19 MOM: You weren't planning on doing something I wouldn't
20   like, were you?
21 MEREDITH: *(Still not sure to believe her good luck)* No, it's
22   just that you don't usually let me have friends over when
23   you're not here.
24 MOM: Well, maybe it's time that I did. I'll let you guys stay
25   alone for two hours. If I get home and the house is still
26   standing and there are no police, that will tell me I
27   should start trusting you more and giving you a little
28   more freedom.
29 MEREDITH: *(Placated)* Wow! That would be awesome! *(Starts*
30   *to leave.)*
31 MOM: Oh, wait! *(MEREDITH stops.)* Is Jake the one whose
32   father owns the bakery?
33 MEREDITH: Yeah.
34 MOM: Would you ask him to bring some of that French
35   bread they make?

1   MEREDITH: *(Appalled)* Mom! I can't ask him that!
2   MOM: Why not? He's getting all the Doritos and Pepsi he
3   can eat and drink. The least he can do is throw in a loaf
4   of French bread.
5   MEREDITH: You're going to drive me crazy, do you know
6   that?
7   MOM: That's the plan.

55. A Good Deed Run Amok

Topic: Trying to do a good deed backfires on a guy who finds a phone.

Cast:

TONY: just trying to be a nice guy
NORRIS: tough, grouchy
GINNY: overly-excited, talks *very* quickly
BECKY: the hurt and angry ex-girlfriend
MOM: a typical mom (or her voicemail, anyway)
DEVIN: the *real* owner of the phone and not particularly friendly or thankful

1　*(TONY crosses the stage and happens across a cell phone on*
2　*the floor. He should stay Center while the others come on*
3　*from opposite sides of the stage. No one should look at TONY.)*
4　**TONY: Hey! Someone must have dropped their phone.**
5　*(Looks around.)* **I wonder whose it is.** *(He opens it, closes*
6　*it, and looks on the back. Pauses.)* **How in the world do I**
7　**find out how to get it back to the owner? I'd die if I lost**
8　**my phone. I know! I'll call the last number on the phone**
9　**and ask them.** *(Dials.)*
10　**NORRIS: Yo.**
11　**TONY:** *(Hesitant but cheerful)* **Oh, uh, hi. I just found this**
12　**phone, and —**
13　**NORRIS: What do you want? You woke me up.**
14　**TONY:** *(A little unsure)* **Oh, sorry. I just wanted to see if you**
15　**could tell me —**
16　**NORRIS:** *(Suspicious)* **Hey, how did you get this number? I**
17　**never give out this number.**
18　**TONY: Well, I found this phone, and —**
19　**NORRIS:** *(Interrupting)* **Is this Spike?**

1   TONY: No, it's Tony.

2   NORRIS: I don't know no Tony.

3   TONY: Yeah, I know. I —

4   NORRIS: *(Interrupting again and angry)* Then whatcha doin'

5   callin' me? And how did you get this number? Did Spike

6   give you my number? Wait 'til I see him.

7   TONY: Is this Spike's phone?

8   NORRIS: *(Pause)* What?

9   TONY: Am I calling from Spike's phone?

10 NORRIS: *(Pause)* How in the world would I know? *You* called

11   me.

12 TONY: You see, I found this phone, and —

13 NORRIS: You tell Spike I said he gives out my number again

14   and I'll get back at him.

15 TONY: No, no, you don't understand. *(NORRIS hangs up.)*

16   Well, that was fun. *(Scrolls through the phone numbers*

17   *again).* Should I try again? I'll try dialing someone on

18   purpose. Here's a promising listing, *Home. (Dials.)*

19 GINNY: Oh, my gosh, you won't believe what happened

20   *(TONY continually tries to interrupt but GINNY won't let him*

21   *get a word in.)* Cynthia Parker told me that Justin McNair

22   told *her* that Bobby Michael likes me! Oh, my gosh, can

23   you believe it? I tried to call Mom on her cell but I think

24   she's in book club and then I called Susie Thomas and

25   she's at an orthodontist appointment. I called Tammy

26   Long, even though I don't like her very much, because

27   she used to like Bobby and I thought she might get

28   jealous. But she didn't answer and, anyway, she isn't all

29   that much fun to talk to. So I was going to call you, but

30   then Sherry called and I told *her* and she said she had

31   already heard from Karen Roberts that Bobby liked me,

32   like last week! I asked her why she didn't tell me and she

33   said she wanted to make sure before she told me

34   because she knows how much I like him and didn't want

35   to tell me if it wasn't true. So now that I know it's true,

1   I've got to call Cammy and Tiffany and Rachel. Bye!
2   *(Hangs up.)*
3 TONY: *(Pauses, looks at phone.)* Man, that tired me out. This
4   poor guy has to live with that? I'll try another number.
5   *(Dials.)*
6 BECKY: *(Obviously angry)* I can't believe you called me.
7 TONY: Hi, um, Becky? This is —
8 BECKY: I know who this is, you jerk. Two weeks without so
9   much as a phone call or e-mail and now you're going to
10   call me the night before the dance.
11 TONY: No, you don't —
12 BECKY: *(Mounting anger)* I don't ever want to talk to you
13   again. You're a jerk and I hate you. Don't ever call me
14   again! *(Hangs up.)*
15 TONY: Don't worry, I won't. *(Stares at the phone for a long*
16   *time.)* I wonder if it's even worth it. *(Dials again.)*
17 MOM: *(Super sweet)* Helloooo! This is Margaret and, guess
18   what? I can't get to the phone. Please leave your name
19   and number and I'll call back. Thank you!
20 TONY: *(Hesitates.)* Uh, Mom? Well, this is Tony. I know you
21   don't know me, and I'm sure you don't have a son
22   named Tony, anyway, I have this phone and your name
23   was on it as Mom so I thought I'd call you to see if you
24   could tell me whose phone it really *is* but then, someone,
25   at home told me you were at book club or something.
26   *(Pauses, obviously confusing himself.)* Anyway, please call
27   this number back and tell me who I am. *(DEVIN walks by,*
28   *sees him with the phone.)*
29 DEVIN: Hey, is that my phone?
30 TONY: Man, I hope so.
31 DEVIN: *(Suspiciously)* What are you doing with my phone?
32 TONY: Are you Spike?
33 DEVIN: Spike? What are you talking about.
34 TONY: Oh, nothing, it's just that Norris thought you might
35   be Spike.

1   DEVIN: Norris? What are you doing, going through my
2   address book?
3   TONY: No, you see, I — *(DEVIN snatches phone away and*
4   *looks at it, scrolling.)*
5   DEVIN: *(Growingly upset)* You called Norris? And my house?
6   And my mother? And ... *Becky?* You called Becky?
7   TONY: *(Quietly, guiltily)* It was the first name on the list.
8   DEVIN: What did she say?
9   TONY: You don't want to know.
10 DEVIN: Shoot, I've been trying to get the nerve up to call her
11   for two weeks. What in the world did you say to her?
12 TONY: I didn't get to say anything. Trust me, though, be
13   glad you didn't call her.
14 DEVIN: I should call the cops for you stealing my phone and
15   invading my privacy or something.
16 TONY: *(Defensively)* I didn't steal your phone! I found it!
17 DEVIN: Yeah, sure. Next time go buy your own stupid phone
18   and keep your nose out of other people's business. You
19   probably ruined my chances with Becky. *(Storms off.)*
20 TONY: I actually think he and Becky would make a great
21   couple.

About the Author

Maggie Scriven began writing skits in the second grade when she discovered that a nice Thanksgiving skit would allow her and her friends to get out of class to perform for other classes. Her love of both writing and drama has continued since then. After raising her three children, Maggie completed her B.S. in English with a minor in drama. She then went on to receive a teaching degree and has continued to work with middle school students. She has been working in local community theatre as an actress and vocal director since her teens and works in drama camps and church drama ministry when possible. Maggie lives in Baltimore with her family.

Maggie would very much like to hear from any groups that are performing these skits, so please contact her at: MagScriven@yahoo.com.

Order Form

Meriwether Publishing Ltd.
PO Box 7710
Colorado Springs, CO 80933-7710
Phone: 800-937-5297   Fax: 719-594-9916
Website: www.meriwether.com

Please send me the following books:

_____ **Short & Sweet Skits for Student Actors** $17.95
#BK-B312
by Maggie Scriven
55 sketches for teens

_____ **Sketch-O-Frenia #BK-B263** $19.95
by John Dessler and Lawrence Phillis
Fifty short and witty satirical sketches

_____ **Improv Ideas #BK-B283** $23.95
by Justine Jones and Mary Ann Kelley
A book and CD-rom of games and lists

_____ **Drama Games and Improvs BK-B296** $22.95
by Justine Jones and Mary Ann Kelley
Games for the classroom and beyond

_____ **Theatre Games for Young Performers** $17.95
#BK-B188
by Maria C. Novelly
Improvisations and exercises for developing acting skills

_____ **More Theatre Games for** $17.95
Young Performers #BK-B268
by Suzi Zimmerman
Improvisations and exercises for developing acting skills

_____ **112 Acting Games #BK-B277** $17.95
by Gavin Levy
A comprehensive workbook of theatre games

These and other fine Meriwether Publishing books are available at your local bookstore or direct from the publisher. Prices subject to change without notice. Check our website or call for current prices.

Name: _____ email: _____

Organization name: _____

Address: _____

City: _____ State: _____

Zip: _____ Phone: _____

❑ **Check enclosed**

❑ **Visa / MasterCard / Discover / Am. Express #** _____

Expiration
Signature: _____ *date:* _____ / _____
          (required for credit card orders)

Colorado residents: Please add 3% sales tax.
Shipping: Include $3.95 for the first book and 75¢ for each additional book ordered.

❑ *Please send me a copy of your complete catalog of books and plays.*

Order Form

Meriwether Publishing Ltd.
PO Box 7710
Colorado Springs, CO 80933-7710
Phone: 800-937-5297 Fax: 719-594-9916
Website: www.meriwether.com

Please send me the following books:

_____ **Short & Sweet Skits for Student Actors** $17.95
#BK-B312
by Maggie Scriven
55 sketches for teens

_____ **Sketch-O-Frenia #BK-B263** $19.95
by John Dessler and Lawrence Phillis
Fifty short and witty satirical sketches

_____ **Improv Ideas #BK-B283** $23.95
by Justine Jones and Mary Ann Kelley
A book and CD-rom of games and lists

_____ **Drama Games and Improvs BK-B296** $22.95
by Justine Jones and Mary Ann Kelley
Games for the classroom and beyond

_____ **Theatre Games for Young Performers** $17.95
#BK-B188
by Maria C. Novelly
Improvisations and exercises for developing acting skills

_____ **More Theatre Games for** $17.95
Young Performers #BK-B268
by Suzi Zimmerman
Improvisations and exercises for developing acting skills

_____ **112 Acting Games #BK-B277** $17.95
by Gavin Levy
A comprehensive workbook of theatre games

**These and other fine Meriwether Publishing books are available at
your local bookstore or direct from the publisher. Prices subject to
change without notice. Check our website or call for current prices.**

Name: _____ email: _____

Organization name: _____

Address: _____

City: _____ State: _____

_____ Phone: _____

▮heck enclosed

▮ / MasterCard / Discover / Am. Express # _____

<table>
<tr><td></td><td>Expiration
date:</td><td>_____ / _____</td></tr>
</table>

_____
(required for credit card orders)

▮esidents: Please add 3% sales tax.
▮Include $3.95 for the first book and 75¢ for each additional book ordered.

▮se send me a copy of your complete catalog of books and plays.